Key Stage 3
Developing Numeracy

ALGEBRA

ACTIVITIES FOR TEACHING NUMERACY

year

Hilary Koll and Steve Mills

A & C BLACK

Contents

Sequences, functions and graphs

Published 2003 by A & C Black Publishers Limited
37 Soho Square, London W1D 3QZ
www.acblack.com

ISBN 0-7136-6473-8

Copyright text © Hilary Koll and Steve Mills, 2003
Copyright illustrations © Brett Hudson, 2003
Copyright cover illustration © Paul Cemmick, 2003
Editors: Lynne Williamson and Marie Lister

The authors and publishers would like to thank David Chadwick, Corinne McCrum and Jane McNeill for their advice in producing this series of books.

A CIP catalogue record for this book is available from the British Library.

Printed in Great Britain by St Edmundsbury Press Ltd, Bury St Edmunds, Suffolk.

A & C Black uses paper produced with elemental chlorine-free pulp, harvested from managed sustainable forests.

Introduction

Key Stage 3 Developing Numeracy: Algebra is a series of photocopiable resources for Years 7, 8 and 9, designed to be used during maths lessons. The books focus on the Algebra strand of the Key Stage 3 National Strategy *Framework for teaching mathematics*.

Each book supports the teaching of mathematics by providing a series of activities that develop essential skills in numeracy. The activities aim to reinforce learning and develop the skills and understanding explored during whole-class teaching. Each task provides practice and consolidation of an objective contained in the framework document. On the whole the activities are designed for pupils to work on independently, either individually or in pairs, although occasionally some pupils may need support.

The activities in **Algebra Year 9** relate to the following topics:

- equations, formulae and identities;
- sequences, functions and graphs.

How to use this book

Each double-page spread is based on a Year 9 objective. The spread has three main sections labelled A, B and C, and ends with a challenge (**Now try this!**). The work grows increasingly difficult from A through to C, and the 'Now try this!' challenge reinforces and extends pupils' learning. The activities provide the teacher with an opportunity to make informal assessments: for example, checking that pupils are developing mental strategies, have grasped the main teaching points, or whether they have any misunderstandings.

This double-page structure can be used in a variety of ways: for example, following whole-class teaching the pupils can begin to work through both sheets and will experience gradually more complex questions, or the teacher can choose the most appropriate starting points for each group in the class, with some pupils starting at A and others at B or C. This allows differentiation for mixed-ability groups. 'Now try this!' provides a greater challenge for more able pupils. It can involve 'Using and Applying' concepts and skills, and provides an opportunity for classroom discussion. Where appropriate, pupils can be asked to finish tasks for homework.

The instructions are presented clearly to enable the pupils to work independently. There are also opportunities for pupils to work in pairs and groups, to encourage discussion and co-operation. A calculator icon indicates whether or not calculators should be used for different parts of the activities. Where there is no icon, the teacher or pupils may choose whether or not to use them. Brief notes are provided at the foot of each page to assist the pupil or classroom assistant, or parent if the sheets are used for homework. Remind the pupils to read these before beginning the activity.

In some cases, the pupils will need to record their workings on a separate piece of paper, and it is suggested that these workings are handed in with the activity sheets. The pupils will also need to record their answers to some of the 'Now try this!' challenges on another piece of paper.

Organisation

Very little equipment is needed, other than the essential rulers, pencils and so on, but for some activity sheets pupils will need algebraic calculators. These activity sheets allow opportunities for pupils to explore keys and interpret the display on the calculator. It is important in some cases that the calculators used have certain keys, for example a sign change key. During the teaching input, discuss how such keys can be shown in different ways on different calculators, for example $\boxed{+/-}$ or $\boxed{(-)}$.

To help teachers select appropriate learning experiences for pupils, the activities are grouped into sections within the book to match the objectives in the Key Stage 3 National Strategy *Yearly teaching programmes*. However, the activities do not have to be used in the order given. The sheets are intended to support, rather than direct, the teacher's planning.

Some activities can be made easier or more challenging by masking or substituting some of the numbers. You may wish to re-use some pages by copying them onto card and laminating them, or by enlarging them onto A3 paper. They could also be made into OHTs for whole-class use.

Teachers' notes

Further brief notes, containing specific instructions or points to be raised during the first part of the lesson, are provided for particular sheets (see pages 6–7).

Whole-class oral and mental starters

The following activities provide some practical ideas to support the main teaching part of the lesson, and can be carried out before pupils use the activity sheets.

Equations, formulae and identities

Rectangle equations

Draw a rectangle on the board and label opposite sides with expressions such as $3x + 4$ and $5x - 6$. Ask the pupils to construct and solve an equation to find the value of x. Once this has been done, the pupils can find the length of the side.

Substitution

Split the class into two teams. Write an equation on the board using the letter x in terms of y: for example, $y = \sqrt{(12 - 3x^2)}$. Each team should roll a dice to generate a value of x to substitute into the equation. Ask them to use a calculator to find the value of y. The answer should be rounded to one or two decimal places and this forms the score for that team. Keep a running total of the scores; the team with the highest score at the end wins. The equations can be changed as often as required.

Identically equal?

Write pairs of expressions on the board: for example, $2(5n + 4n - 6)$ and $18n - 6$. Remind the pupils that identically equal expressions are equivalent whatever the value of the letter, and ask them to say whether or not the expressions on the board are identically equal. Encourage the pupils to make up their own 'identically equal' puzzles for the rest of the class to solve.

How old?

Write some 'How old?' puzzles on the board which have algebraic answers, for example:

I am x years older than my brother. He was half my age y years ago. How old am I now?

Colin is p years old. q years ago his brother was three-quarters of his age. How old is his brother now?

Ask the pupils to write and simplify an expression to answer each question.

Rows and columns

Draw a grid similar to the one below and write an expression in each box using the letters x and y. Ask the pupils to find the totals of the expressions in each row and column. Encourage them to predict which row or column will have the greatest/fewest number of 'x's, or the greatest/fewest number of 'y's.

$3x - y$	$2x$	$y - 4x$	$3y + 2x$
$2y$	$3x - y$	$3y + x$	$2x - 5y$
$2x + 4y$	$2x - 2y$	$y - x$	$4y + 3x$
$y - 4x$	$6y - x$	$x - 5y$	x

Sequences, functions and graphs

Pattern spotting

Choose a rule to show a relationship between values of x and y: for example, $y = 4x - 1$. Do not reveal it to the class. Draw a table on the board for several values of x (for example, $^-3$, $^-2$, $^-1$, 0, 1, 2, 3) and fill in the corresponding values of y. Invite the pupils to spot the relationship between the values of x and y. When pupils think they have spotted the pattern, invite them to add another pair of values to the table that fits the rule (without saying what the rule is). Once most pupils have spotted the pattern, invite one of them to write the rule on the board as an equation. The coordinates could then be plotted to show that they make a straight line.

Guess the equation of the line

On the board, draw a coordinate grid labelled $^-4$ to 4. Choose an equation: for example, $y = x$ or $x = ^-2$. Do not reveal it to the class. Invite the pupils to give pairs of coordinates on the grid. For each pair of coordinates, say whether it is a 'hit' (if it lies along your line) or a 'miss'. Encourage the pupils to guess the equation of the line by looking at the pairs of coordinates that are 'hits'. The pupils could provide further pairs of coordinates that lie along the line (including fractional ones) once they have found the correct equation.

Teachers' notes

Equations, formulae and identities

Pages 8 & 9

These pages help the pupils to appreciate that both sides of an inequality can be added to, subtracted from, and multiplied or divided by a positive number, and the inequality remains true. However, when multiplying and dividing both sides by a negative number, the inequality sign must be reversed to make it true. Encourage the pupils to test inequalities by substituting appropriate values.

Pages 10 & 11

Pupils often take time to realise the different ways in which letters are used in algebra and in what situations two expressions are equal. Two expressions can be equal for a particular value of the letter, or can be equal whatever the value of the letter. If they are equal whatever the value of the letter or letters, the expressions are said to be identically equal and the identity sign ($\equiv$) can be used. The pupils should be encouraged to discuss their findings with a partner. Invite them to share their observations during the plenary session.

Pages 12 & 13

These pages explore the index laws. Encourage the pupils to discover the index laws by observation rather than just teaching them the rules of adding and subtracting powers when multiplying and dividing.

Revise the difference between multiplying indices, for example $n^2 \times n^2$, and adding them, for example $n^2 + n^2$. To emphasise this, rewrite n^2 as $n \times n$ and show that $n^2 \times n^2$ is $n \times n \times n \times n = n^4$, whereas $n^2 + n^2$ is $(n \times n) + (n \times n) = 2(n \times n) = 2n^2$.

Pages 14 & 15

When finding the difference between two expressions in part B, the pupils will need to understand the effect of a subtraction sign outside a set of brackets, for example $- 3(4a - b)$. Discuss how the expression $- 3(4a - b)$ is identically equal to $- 12a + 3b$, demonstrating how $^-3 \times {}^-b$ gives positive $3b$. Remind the pupils that a negative number multiplied or divided by a negative number gives a positive number. This and other related rules can be summarised as:

negative × negative = positive
negative ÷ negative = positive
positive × negative = negative
positive ÷ negative = negative
negative × positive = negative
negative ÷ positive = negative

Pages 16 & 17

The activities on these pages explore using the lowest common multiple (LCM) to help add and subtract algebraic fractions with different denominators. When dealing with numerical fractions, the sum or difference can be found by changing each fraction to an equivalent one with the LCM as the denominator, and then adding or subtracting the numerators.

Demonstrate to the pupils how, when adding numerical or algebraic fractions with different denominators, it is necessary to change the fractions so that they have the same denominator. To determine which new denominator to use, the pupils should find the lowest common multiple (LCM) of the existing denominators: for example, $\frac{1}{a} + \frac{3}{b} + \frac{5}{c}$ can be found by changing each fraction to an equivalent one with the LCM (abc) as the denominator.

Pages 18 & 19

Part C explores different ways of describing the area of a shaded part of a rectangle. One way is to find the area of the large rectangle and subtract the area of the smaller (unshaded) rectangle. A second way is to split the shaded part into two rectangles by drawing a vertical line. A third way is to split the shaded part into two rectangles by drawing a horizontal line. Expressions should be written for each way. The pupils should appreciate and be able to show that the different expressions are identically equal.

Pages 20 & 21

There are two main ways of solving simple equations: using inverses and using ideas of balance. The pupils can use either method for the activities on these pages. They will encounter negative values in both questions and solutions.

Pages 22 & 23

Some pupils may be able to solve some of the problems in parts A and B without constructing and using linear equations. They should, however, be encouraged to use such a method, as it can help them to solve more complex problems and puzzles. Before tackling part C, revise that the angles along a straight line and the sum of the interior angles of a triangle equal 180°, and that angles about a point and the sum of the angles in a quadrilateral equal 360°.

Pages 24 & 25

Encourage the pupils to check their solutions by entering the value of the letter into the equation, and checking that both sides of the equals sign have the same value.

Pages 26–29

These pages introduce methods of trial and improvement. The pupils will need to be confident in ordering decimals before they begin. Remind them to compare the digits of decimals in turn, beginning with the most significant digit – the one on the left.

Discuss giving answers, where necessary, to two decimal places. Revise rounding to the nearest hundredth.

Pages 30 & 31

Begin the lesson by reminding the pupils that things are in direct proportion when they increase in the same ratio (for example, the number of litres of petrol you can buy for given numbers of pounds). The pupils will require squared paper for part B.

Pages 32 & 33

It is possible to make different words when rearranging the letters, but pupils should be able to make a sensible sentence with each word. Encourage them to make up their own simple code games in the same way.

Pages 34 & 35

In the 'Now try this!' challenge, discuss how the subject can be changed using inverses: for example, $\frac{9C}{5} + 32 = F$ can be written as the flow diagram:

$C \rightarrow \times 9 \rightarrow \div 5 \rightarrow + 32 = F$

In reverse this is:

$C = \div 9 \leftarrow \times 5 \leftarrow - 32 \leftarrow F$

which is $\frac{5}{9}(F - 32) = C$.

Pages 36 & 37

Encourage the pupils to use inverses when rearranging formulae. Some pupils may find it useful to write out the formulae using operation signs (for example, writing $V = IR$ as $V = I \times R$ or $V = R \times I$). This can help them to analyse which inverse operation is necessary to make R or I the subject of the formula.

Sequences, functions and graphs

Pages 40 & 41

Explain that an arithmetic sequence (one where adjacent terms have a constant difference) can be described in two ways: using a term-to-term rule and a position-to-term rule. The term-to-term rule describes how each term is related to the previous term in the sequence. The position-to-term rule describes each term in relation to its position in the sequence. The latter is more useful in predicting other terms of the sequence.

Pages 42 & 43

Each pair will require a dice and a counter for the game in part C.

Pages 44 & 45

Here, pupils are introduced to quadratic sequences where the first difference increases by a constant amount each time. The pupils are encouraged to notice that for linear sequences such as $5n + 3$, the first difference is constant (for example, adjacent terms have a difference of 5 each time). During the plenary session discuss how, for quadratic sequences, the number of n^2 is half the second difference: for example, $4n^2$ has a second difference of 8.

Pages 46 & 47

These pages encourage the pupils to appreciate shape sequences and to see a link between the visual representation and the position-to-term rule. Discuss how for some sequences, part of the shape or model of each term remains constant, whilst another part grows. Refer to the example on page 46 part A, where the number of grey squares remains the same (1), whilst each of the two 'legs' grows by 1 each time. Draw attention to the fact that, in the position-to-term rule for this sequence ($2n + 1$), the grey square is the $+ 1$ part of the rule and the two 'legs' are the $2n$ part.

Pages 48 & 49

The pupils will require squared paper for part B.

Pages 50 & 51

Demonstrate simple mapping diagrams at the start of the lesson. Discuss how functions can be written in two ways: for example, $x \rightarrow 3(x + 2)$ or $y = 3(x + 2)$. Explore the inverse of this function: $x \rightarrow \frac{x}{3} - 2$. When writing inverse functions, encourage the pupils to check by applying the original function to numbers such as 1, 2, 3 and 4, then applying the inverse function to the output values to see whether they give the numbers 1, 2, 3 and 4.

Pages 52 & 53

For part C, the pupils will need a graphical calculator or ICT to develop and explore graphs of functions.

Pages 54 & 55

The pupils will require squared paper for parts B and C.

Inequality inquiry

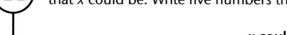

A

For each | inequality |, write five numbers (integers or decimals)
that x could be. Write five numbers that x could not be.

x could be   **x could not be**

(a) $x < 7$ | 6.5 | ⁻8 | | | | | 7 | 10.2 | | | |

(b) $x > 2$

(c) $x \geq {}^-3$

(d) $x \leq {}^-5$

(e) $0 < x \leq 1$

(f) $^-5 \leq x \leq {}^-4$

B

For each inequality, follow the instruction and write a new inequality. Then choose a value
for y that satisfies the *first* inequality. Use it to test whether the second inequality is true.

(a) | $y > 7$ | ——— Add 4 to both sides ——→ | $y + 4 > 11$ |

   Test: y could be 10 $10 + 4 > 11$
                                                  $14 > 11$ True

(b) | $y \leq 4$ | ——— Subtract 3 from both sides ——→ | $y - 3 \leq 1$ |

(c) | $y + 6 \geq 7$ | ——— Subtract 6 from both sides ——→ | |

(d) | $y > {}^-4$ | ——— Add 10 to both sides ——→ | |

(e) | $y + 1 \leq 1.5$ | ——— Subtract 5 from both sides ——→ | |

An **inequality** is a statement that one expression is greater than or less
than another. The sign $\geq$ means 'greater than or equal to' (for example,
$x \geq 7$ means 'x is greater than or equal to 7'). The sign $\leq$ means 'less than
or equal to' (for example, $x \leq {}^-4$ means 'x is less than or equal to $^-4$').

Developing Numeracy
Algebra
Year 9
© A & C BLACK

Inequality inquiry

1. For each **inequality**, follow the instruction and write a new inequality. Then choose a value for *y* that satisfies the *first* inequality. Use it to test whether the second inequality is true.

(a) | $y > 6$ | —— Multiply both sides by 2 ——▶ | $2y > 12$ |

Test: *y could be 10*

$$2 \times 10 > 12$$
$$20 > 12 \qquad True$$

(b) | $y \leq 4$ | —— Multiply both sides by 5 ——▶ |  |

(c) | $y \geq 35$ | —— Divide both sides by 5 ——▶ |  |

(d) | $y > 5$ | —— Multiply both sides by ⁻2 ——▶ |  |

(e) | $y \leq 2$ | —— Multiply both sides by ⁻1 ——▶ |  |

(f) | $y \leq 16$ | —— Divide both sides by ⁻4 ——▶ |  |

(g) | $y \leq {}^-1$ | —— Divide both sides by ⁻1 ——▶ |  |

2. Write what you notice about multiplying and dividing inequalities by negative numbers.

_____

NOW TRY THIS!

- Use your explanation to help you complete these inequalities.

  (a) If ⁻e < ⁻9, then e _____

  (b) If ⁻f ≥ 1, then f _____

- Make up four similar inequalities for a partner to solve.

An **inequality** is a statement that one expression is greater than or less than another. The sign ≥ means 'greater than or equal to'. The sign ≤ means 'less than or equal to'. In the 'Now try this!' challenge, check your answers by replacing the letter in the expressions with a number. Try out the largest possible numbers and the smallest to check your answers.

Developing Numeracy
Algebra
Year 9
© A & C BLACK

Identity parade

A

1. (a) Complete the table for these expressions.

$2a + 8$ $3(a + 2)$

(b) For what value(s) of a are the two expressions equal? _____

Value of a	$2a + 8$	$3(a + 2)$
1	10	9
2		
3		
4		
5		

2. (a) Complete the table for these expressions.

$2(a + 3)$ $2a + 6$

(b) For what value(s) of a are the two expressions equal? _____

Value of a	$2(a + 3)$	$2a + 6$
1		
2		
3		
4		
5		

B

For each pair of expressions, only one speech bubble is correct. Tick it.

(a) $4y - 8$ $3y - 2$

Whatever the value of **y** is, these two expressions are equal. ☐

Only when **y** = 6 are these two expressions equal. ☐

(b) $4(a + 1)$ $4a + 4$

Whatever the value of **a** is, these two expressions are equal. ☐

Only when **a** = 5 are these two expressions equal. ☐

(c) $7x - 7$ $3(x + x)$

Whatever the value of **x** is, these two expressions are equal. ☐

Only when **x** = 7 are these two expressions equal. ☐

(d) $6b - 3b$ $2b + b$

Whatever the value of **b** is, these two expressions are equal. ☐

Only when **b** = 2 are these two expressions equal. ☐

(e) $3s + 7$ $6s - 5$

Whatever the value of **s** is, these two expressions are equal. ☐

Only when **s** = 4 are these two expressions equal. ☐

(f) $2(7 - p)$ $14 - p$

Whatever the value of **p** is, these two expressions are equal. ☐

Only when **p** = 0 are these two expressions equal. ☐

Letters can be used in different ways. Sometimes a letter stands for an unknown number that you have to find (for example, $n + 2 = 5$). Sometimes a letter stands for any number you choose (for example, $n + 3 = ?$). In other expressions, the value of one letter depends on the value of another (for example, $x + y = 9$; if y equals 2 then x must equal 7).

Developing Numeracy
Algebra
Year 9
© A & C BLACK

Identity parade

C

1. For each equation, say whether or not the expressions are ⬜ identically equal . If they are *not* identically equal, this means that they are only equal for a particular value of *n*.

(a) $2(n + 1) = 2n + 2$

identically equal

(b) $3n + 4 = 4n - 2$

not identically equal

(c) $4(n + 2) = 4n + 8$

(d) $5n = 2n + 6$

(e) $n \times n \times n = n^3$

(f) $3(2n - n) = 3n$

(g) $4n - 4 = 2(n + 1)$

(h) $4(n + 1) = 4n + 4$

(i) $3n + 0 = 4n - n$

(j) $5(2 - n) = 10 - n$

2. For each equation above where the expressions are identically equal, write an ⬜ identity . Use the identity sign ⬜ ≡ between the expressions.

$2(n + 1) \equiv 2n + 2$

3. In these boxes, write the equations from question 1 where the expressions are **not** identically equal. Find the value of *n* which makes the expressions equal.

$3n + 4 = 4n - 2$

is only true when n = 6

- Write four identities of your own, using the identity sign ⬜ ≡ . Discuss your identically equal expressions with a partner.

Identically equal expressions are expressions that will always be equal whatever values are used for the letters. An **identity** uses the identity sign (≡) to show that the expressions on each side of the equation are identically equal: for example, $4(n + 1) \equiv 4n + 4$.

Developing Numeracy
Algebra
Year 9
© A & C BLACK

11

Power play

A Answer these questions.

(a) $n^2 \times n^3 = \underline{(n \times n) \times (n \times n \times n) = n \times n \times n \times n \times n = n^5}$

(b) $a^4 \times a^3 = $

(c) $c^2 \times c^4 = $

(d) $y^6 \times y^2 = $

(e) $b^4 \div b^2 = \dfrac{(b \times b \times \cancel{b}^1 \times \cancel{b}^1)}{(\cancel{b}^1 \times \cancel{b}^1)} = \dfrac{b \times b}{1} = b^2$

(f) $x^5 \div x^2 = $

(g) $m^4 \div m^3 = $

(h) $d^6 \div d^4 = $

B **1.** Follow the instructions. Write questions and find the answers using the templates below.

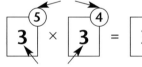

Write one-digit numbers in the circles.

To find the answer, add the **powers**.

$3^{(5)} \times 3^{(4)} = 3^{(9)}$

Write the same letter or number in each box.

This number or letter stays the same.

(a) $4^{(2)} \times 4^{(3)} = 4^{(5)}$

(b) $8^{(2)} \times 8^{(4)} = $

(c) $\square \times \square = \square$

(d) $\square \times \square = \square$

(e) $\square \times \square = \square$

(f) $\square \times \square = \square$

(g) $\square \times \square = \square$

(h) $\square \times \square = \square$

(i) $\square \times \square = \square$

2. Evaluate the answer to each of your questions above.

Evaluate means 'give the value of'.

 Remember that the **power** tells you how many of a number are multiplied together: for example, 4^3 ('four to the power three' or 'four cubed') is the same as $4 \times 4 \times 4$. To **evaluate** your answers, work out their value: for example, 'evaluate 4^2' means 'give the value of 4^2', which is 16.

Developing Numeracy
Algebra
Year 9
© A & C BLACK

Power play

1. Follow the instructions. Write questions and find the answers using the templates below.

Write one-digit numbers in the circles.

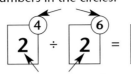

Write the same number or letter in each box.

To find the answer, subtract the second **power** from the first.

This number or letter stays the same.

$$3^{\boxed{7}} \div 3^{\boxed{2}} = 3^{\boxed{5}}$$

2. Simplify these expressions.

(a) $\dfrac{3^7}{3^2}$ = 3^5

(b) $\dfrac{7^8}{7^3}$ = _____

(c) $\dfrac{a^6}{a^5}$ = _____

(d) $\dfrac{9^6}{9^2}$ = _____

(e) $\dfrac{d^8}{d^6}$ = _____

(f) $\dfrac{x^9}{x^5}$ = _____

(g) $\dfrac{3^4 \times 3^3}{3^5}$ = $\dfrac{3^7}{3^5} = 3^2$

(h) $\dfrac{6^4 \times 6^6}{6^9}$ = _____

(i) $\dfrac{4^6 \times 4^6}{4^7}$ = _____

(j) $\dfrac{2^6 \times 2^4}{2^3}$ = _____

(k) $\dfrac{8^4 \times 8^8}{8^9}$ = _____

(l) $\dfrac{5^3 \times 5^6}{5^5}$ = _____

(m) $\dfrac{4^2 \times 4^2}{4^4}$ = _____

(n) $\dfrac{a^4 \times a^6}{a^3}$ = _____

(o) $\dfrac{b^4 \times b^5}{b^{10}}$ = _____

(p) $\dfrac{c^5 \times c^2}{c^3 \times c^3}$ = _____

(q) $\dfrac{y^3 \times y^3}{y^5 \times y^2}$ = _____

(r) $\dfrac{n^4 \times n^5}{n^9 \times n^2}$ = _____

NOW TRY THIS!

• Write the units digit of each of these powers of four.

	4^2	4^3	4^4	4^5	4^6	4^7	4^8	4^9	4^{10}
Units digit	6								

 What do you notice?

• Use what you have noticed to find the units digits of: **(a)** 4^{20} _____ **(b)** 4^{21} _____

 Remember that the **power** tells you how many of a number are multiplied together: for example, $4^3 = 4 \times 4 \times 4$. Where an expression has a higher power beneath the division line than above it, you still need to subtract the bottom number from the top number: for example, $\frac{n^2}{n^3} = n^{-1}$. Note that n^{-1} is the same as $\frac{1}{n}$, n^{-2} is the same as $\frac{1}{n^2}$, and so on.

Developing Numeracy
Algebra
Year 9
© A & C BLACK

13

Multiply then simplify

A

1. Expand the brackets in these expressions.

(a) $3(a + b) =$ _3a + 3b_ **(b)** $5(a + 4) =$ _____ **(c)** $7(8 + b) =$ _____

(d) $x(y + z) =$ _____ **(e)** $a(b + 9) =$ _____ **(f)** $5(a - 4) =$ _____

(g) $4(x - y) =$ _____ **(h)** $9(7 - b) =$ _____ **(i)** $a(a - 3) =$ _____

2. Factorise these expressions. Find a factor and write it outside the brackets.

(a) $3a + 6 =$ _3(a + 2)_ **(b)** $4a + 8 =$ _____ **(c)** $5d + 15e =$ _____

(d) $9c + 6d =$ _____ **(e)** $2x + 8y =$ _____ **(f)** $10p + 10q =$ _____

(g) $4a - 12b =$ _____ **(h)** $x^2 - x =$ _____ **(i)** $10s - 8t =$ _____

(j) $15x - 5x^2 =$ _____ **(k)** $6t - 6 =$ _____ **(l)** $8g - 18g^2 =$ _____

B Find the sum of the expressions in each pair. Then find the difference between them. Expand the brackets first.

(a) $3(a + 2b)$ $4(2a + b)$

Sum _(3a + 6b) + (8a + 4b)_
_11a + 10b_

Difference _(3a + 6b) - (8a + 4b)_
_⁻5a + 2b_

(b) $4(c + 3d)$ $5(2c + d)$

Sum _____

Difference _____

(c) $5(x - 3y)$ $4(3x + 2y)$

Sum _____

Difference _____

(d) $3(4s + 5t)$ $7(s - 2t)$

Sum _____

Difference _____

(e) $6(a - 5b)$ $3(4a - b)$

Sum _____

Difference _____

(f) $5(3m - 2n)$ $6(4m - 3n)$

Sum _____

Difference _____

 To **factorise** an expression, look at the terms in the expression and find a factor (a number or letter that you can divide both terms by). Write the factor outside the brackets. Check your answer by expanding the brackets.

Developing Numeracy
Algebra
Year 9
© A & C BLACK

Multiply then simplify

C

1. Write the area of each stamp *without* using brackets.

(a)

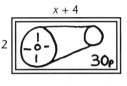

$x + 4$

2

30p

Area = $2x + 8$

(b)

$x + 2$

x

60p

Area = _____

(c)

$2x + 3$

3

34p

Area = _____

(d)

$x - 3$

x

40p

Area = _____

(e)

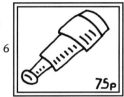

$2x - 6$

6

75p

Area = _____

(f)

$3x - 7$

x

£1

Area = _____

(g)

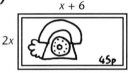

$x + 6$

2x

45p

Area = _____

(h)

$2x + 2$

3x

80p

Area = _____

(i)

$4x - 6$

5x

90p

Area = _____

2. The area of each stamp is given. Write the length of the stamp.

(a)

$x + 6$

x

50p

Area = $x^2 + 6x$

(b)

_____

4

30p

Area = $4x + 4$

(c)

_____

3x

80p

Area = $3x^2 + 6x$

(d)

_____

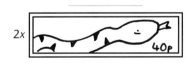

2x

40p

Area = $2x^2 + 8x$

(e)

_____

5

70p

Area = $10x - 5$

(f)

_____

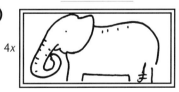

4x

£1

Area = $12x^2 - 8x$

NOW TRY THIS!

- Write at least four different sets of lengths and widths for this stamp.

Area = $4x^2 + 8x$

65p

When you multiply two expressions, remember to multiply both parts of the second expression by the first (for example, $2x$ multiplied by $x + 4$ gives $2x^2 + 8x$).

Developing Numeracy
Algebra
Year 9
© A & C BLACK

Fraction fracas

A

1. What is the | lowest common multiple | (**LCM**) of:

(a) 7 and 6? _42_

(b) 4 and 7? _____

(c) 3 and 8? _____

(d) 5 and 7? _____

(e) 9 and 10? _____

(f) 4 and 9? _____

(g) a and b? _____

(h) c and d? _____

(i) e and f? _____

2. Change these fractions to equivalent ones.

> Multiply the numerator and the denominator by the same value. **!**

(a) $\dfrac{2}{7} = \dfrac{}{42}$

(b) $\dfrac{3}{4} = \dfrac{}{28}$

(c) $\dfrac{6}{7} = \dfrac{}{35}$

(d) $\dfrac{7}{9} = \dfrac{}{36}$

(e) $\dfrac{2}{a} = \dfrac{}{ab}$

(f) $\dfrac{3}{b} = \dfrac{}{ab}$

(g) $\dfrac{7}{c} = \dfrac{}{cd}$

(h) $\dfrac{1}{d} = \dfrac{}{cd}$

(i) $\dfrac{a}{b} = \dfrac{}{ab}$

B

Use the LCM to help you add these fractions.

(a) $\dfrac{1}{8} + \dfrac{3}{4} = \dfrac{(1 \times 4) + (3 \times 8)}{32} = \dfrac{4 + 24}{32} = \dfrac{28}{32} = \dfrac{7}{8}$

(b) $\dfrac{1}{5} + \dfrac{4}{7} = \dfrac{(1 \times) + (4 \times)}{35} = \dfrac{}{} = \dfrac{}{}$

(c) $\dfrac{2}{3} + \dfrac{3}{8} = \dfrac{(2 \times) + (3 \times)}{} = \dfrac{}{} = \dfrac{}{} = \dfrac{}{}$

(d) $\dfrac{3}{5} + \dfrac{1}{4} = \dfrac{}{} = \dfrac{}{} = \dfrac{}{}$

(e) $\dfrac{1}{a} + \dfrac{2}{b} = \dfrac{(1 \times) + (2 \times)}{ab} = \dfrac{}{}$

(f) $\dfrac{2}{c} + \dfrac{3}{d} = \dfrac{}{cd} = \dfrac{}{}$

The **LCM** of several numbers is the lowest number into which all the numbers will divide. Remember that you can multiply the numerator and denominator of any fraction by the same value and the new fraction will be equivalent: for example, the fraction $\frac{2}{b}$ can be multiplied by a on both the top and bottom to make the equivalent fraction $\frac{2a}{ab}$.

Developing Numeracy
Algebra
Year 9
© A & C BLACK

C

1. Use the **lowest common multiple (LCM)** to help you add and subtract these fractions.

(a) $\dfrac{3}{a} - \dfrac{1}{b} = \dfrac{(3 \times b) - (1 \times a)}{ab} = \dfrac{3b - a}{ab}$

> ! Use the denominators to find the lowest common multiple.

(b) $\dfrac{4}{a} + \dfrac{3}{b} = \dfrac{(4 \times) + (3 \times)}{ab} = \dfrac{}{ab}$

(c) $\dfrac{5}{c} + \dfrac{2}{d} = \underline{} = \underline{}$

(d) $\dfrac{6}{c} - \dfrac{3}{d} = \underline{} = \underline{}$

(e) $\dfrac{a}{c} + \dfrac{b}{d} = \underline{} = \underline{}$

(f) $\dfrac{a}{c} - \dfrac{b}{d} = \underline{} = \underline{}$

2. Play this game with a partner.

☆ Take it in turns for one player to be 'Sum' and the other to be 'Difference'.

☆ Each player chooses a fraction from the goal.

☆ The 'Sum' player finds the sum of the two fractions. The 'Difference' player finds the difference between them. Record both calculations.

☆ Now check each other's answers.

☆ Score a point if your answer appears on a ball.

☆ The winner is the first player with four points.

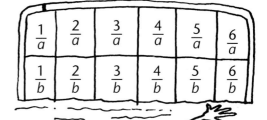

NOW TRY THIS!

• Find the sum of each pair of fractions. Then find the difference.

(a) $\dfrac{a}{c}$ $\dfrac{a}{d}$

(b) $\dfrac{2b}{c}$ $\dfrac{b}{d}$

(c) $\dfrac{d}{c}$ $\dfrac{c}{d}$

The **LCM** of several numbers is the lowest number into which all the numbers will divide. To add or subtract fractions, change the fractions to equivalent ones so that the denominators are the same. For the game in part C, remember that each difference can be written in two ways: for example, $\frac{1}{a} - \frac{2}{b} = \frac{b - 2a}{ab}$ or $\frac{2}{b} - \frac{1}{a} = \frac{2a - b}{ab}$.

Can you prove it?

Prove these statements. Use the letter *n* to stand for the first consecutive integer.
Use *n* + 1, *n* + 2, and so on to stand for the other integers.

(a)

> If you add three consecutive integers, the answer will always be a multiple of 3.

(b)

> If you add five consecutive integers, the answer will always be a multiple of 5.

(c)

> If you add seven consecutive integers, the answer will always be a multiple of 7.

(d)

> If you take two consecutive integers, square them and then find the difference, the answer will be odd.

B

Each of these puzzles ends with its starting number. To show why each puzzle works, write an expression using the letter *n* to stand for the number. Then simplify it.

(a) Think of a number, add 5, multiply by 2, subtract 8, divide by 2 and then subtract 1.

$$\frac{2(n+5)-8}{2} - 1 = \frac{2n+10-8}{2} - 1$$
$$= n + 1 - 1 = n$$

(b) Think of a number, subtract 1, multiply by 4, add 12, divide by 4 and then subtract 2.

(c) Think of a number, multiply by 5, subtract 1, multiply by 2, add 2 and then divide by 10.

(d) Think of a number, add 4, multiply by 6, subtract 20, divide by 2, subtract 2 and then divide by 3.

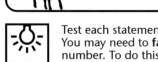

Test each statement first by trying examples. Then use algebra to prove it.
You may need to **factorise** the expression to prove that it is divisible by a
number. To do this, rewrite the expression with the number outside a pair
of brackets: for example, write 3*n* + 3 as 3(*n* + 1) to show that it is divisible
by 3.

Developing Numeracy
Algebra
Year 9
© A & C BLACK

Can you prove it?

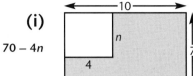

C

The area of the shaded part of this rectangle can be expressed in three ways.

(i) Find the area of the large rectangle, then subtract the area of the small rectangle from it.

(ii) and **(iii)** Split the shaded area into two rectangles and add the areas. (This can be done in two different ways.)

(i) $70 - 4n$

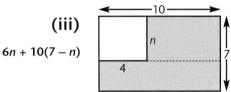

(ii) $42 + 4(7 - n)$

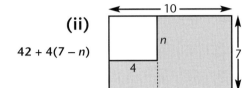

(iii) $6n + 10(7 - n)$

1. Simplify expressions **(ii)** and **(iii)** to show that they are equivalent to expression **(i)**.

(a) $42 + 4(7 - n)$ **(b)** $6n + 10(7 - n)$

_____   _____

_____   _____

Remember to use **BODMAS**.

2. Write the area of the shaded part in all three ways. Prove that your three expressions are equivalent by simplifying.

Proof

(a)

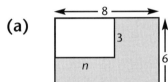

_____

_____

_____

_____

(b)

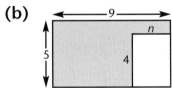

_____

_____

_____

(c)

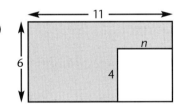

_____

_____

_____

(d)

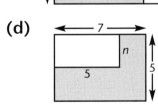

_____

_____

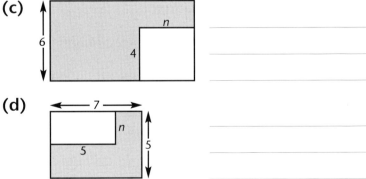

• Use algebra to prove that the square of any odd number will always be odd. Use the expression $2n + 1$ to stand for the odd number.

 Use subtraction to find the measurements you need to know: for example, if the large rectangle has a width of 7 and part of this length measures 'n', then the rest of this side measures $7 - n$. Remember the order of **BODMAS**: do the brackets first, then other things such as squaring, then do multiplication and division, and do addition and subtraction last.

R U positive?

A Use an appropriate method to solve these equations.

(a) $4b + 15 = 3$	**(b)** $5x + 12 = 2$	**(c)** $6x - 16 = 8$	**(d)** $2t - 9 = {}^-7$
(e) $5n - 2 = {}^-27$	**(f)** $3(g - 6) = 12$	**(g)** $5(a - 4) = {}^-50$	**(h)** $6(c + 8) = 6$
(i) $8(m + 4) = {}^-8$	**(j)** $21 = 7(n + 6)$	**(k)** ${}^-108 = 9(h - 10)$	**(l)** ${}^-16 = 8(7 + k)$

B This puzzle can be solved easily using algebra.

The sum of four consecutive integers is 210. What are the integers?

Let n be the first integer, $n + 1$ the second, and so on.

$n + (n + 1) + (n + 2) + (n + 3) = 210$ 　　　 $4n + 6 = 210$
　　　　　　　　　　　　　　　　　　　　　　 $4n = 204$
　　　　　　　　　　　　　　　　　　　　　　 $n = 51$

The integers are 51, 52, 53 and 54.

Solve these puzzles to find the integers.

(a) The sum of four consecutive integers is 82.

$4n + 6 = 82$

The integers are ____ ____ ____

(b) The sum of three consecutive integers is 105.

The integers are ____ ____ ____

(c) The sum of five consecutive integers is 140.

The integers are ____ ____ ____ ____

(d) The sum of five consecutive integers is ‾195.

The integers are ____ ____ ____ ____

Remember that a letter can stand for a positive or negative number. In part A, you can solve the equations using inverse operations or by doing the same to both sides of the equals sign to make the equation balance. Remember that $6a$ means $6 \times a$. Check your solutions by replacing the letter in the equation with the value you have worked out.

Developing Numeracy
Algebra
Year 9
© A & C BLACK

R U positive?

C **1.** Solve these equations.

(a) $4(c - 1) + 5(c - 1) = 18$

(b) $3(b + 2) + 4(b - 3) = {}^-20$

(c) $4(a + 3) - 3(a + 5) = {}^-6$

(d) $3(y + 1) + 2(y - 3) = {}^-28$

(e) $5(p + 1) - 2(p + 9) = {}^-1$

(f) $3(m + 8) - 2(m - 2) = 24$

(g) $6(3 + n) - 5(8 - n) = 0$

(h) $7(8 - s) - 4(7 - s) = 55$

2.

☆ Find the sum of the expressions in each row and column. Simplify your answers.

☆ Then solve the equations to find the values of a, b and c.

$a =$ ☐ $b =$ ☐ $c =$ ☐

☆ Check your answers by substituting the values into each expression. Check that each row and column totals **36**.

$3(a + 1)$	$6 - a$	$7a - 9$	$= 36$
$5 - b$	$8 - 6b$	$b - 7$	$= 36$
$10 - c$	$5c + 1$	$25 - 4c$	$= 36$
$= 36$	$= 36$	$= 36$	

NOW TRY THIS!

The value of the expression at the top of the pyramid is $^-$**48**.

● Find the value of the expression in each box. Check that the sum of adjacent boxes is written in the box above.

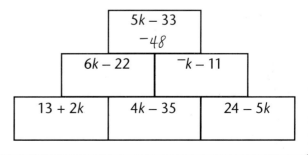

For question 2, work on a separate piece of paper. Add and simplify the expressions in each of the first two rows, then write each answer equal to 36. Solve the equations to find the values of a and b. Then use the columns to find the value of c.

Developing Numeracy
Algebra
Year 9
© A & C BLACK
21

Clever construction

A Construct and simplify ⟨linear equations⟩ to help you solve these problems.

(a) Ali is 3 years younger than his brother.
The sum of their ages is 25.
How old is Ali?

$\overbrace{\text{Ali's age}}$ $\overbrace{\text{His brother's age}}$

$a + (a + 3) = 25$
$2a + 3 = 25$
$2a = 22$, so $a = 11$

(b) Ben is 7 years younger than his sister.
The sum of their ages is 23.
How old is Ben?

(c) Colin is 4 years older than his sister.
The sum of their ages is 16.
How old is Colin?

(d) Dec is 9 years older than his sister.
The sum of their ages is 21.
How old is Dec?

B Bill Derr, Doug Down and Tim Burr work on a building site. Each day they share a large bag of sweets. How many sweets does each worker eat each day?

(a) 67 sweets were eaten.
Bill ate 9 more than Tim.
Doug ate 5 fewer than Tim.
Tim ate the rest.

$\overbrace{\text{Tim}}$ $\overbrace{\text{Bill}}$ $\overbrace{\text{Doug}}$

$t + (t + 9) + (t - 5) = 67$
$3t + 4 = 67$
$3t = 63$, $t = 21$
Tim 21, Bill 30, Doug 16 (= total 67)

(b) 47 sweets were eaten.
Bill ate 3 more than Tim.
Doug ate 7 fewer than Tim.
Tim ate the rest.

(c) 50 sweets were eaten.
Bill ate 6 fewer than Tim.
Doug ate 8 more than Tim.
Tim ate the rest.

(d) 42 sweets were eaten.
Bill ate 8 fewer than Tim.
Doug ate 4 fewer than Tim.
Tim ate the rest.

A **linear equation** is one that does not use squared or cubed values. In each question in part B, write an equation using the letter t to stand for the number of sweets Tim ate. Simplify and solve the equation to find the value of t, then use this to find the number of sweets eaten by the other two men.

Developing Numeracy
Algebra
Year 9
© A & C BLACK

Clever construction

C

1. Construct and simplify **linear equations** to help you find the angles of these triangles.

(a)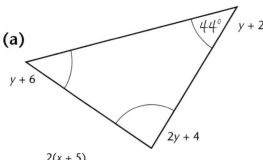
$44°$ $y + 2$
$y + 6$
$2y + 4$

(b)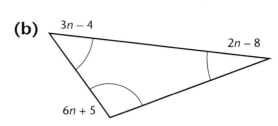
$3n - 4$
$2n - 8$
$6n + 5$

(c)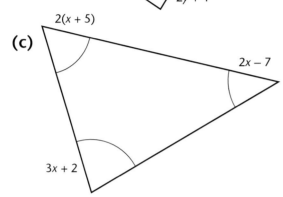
$2(x + 5)$
$2x - 7$
$3x + 2$

(d)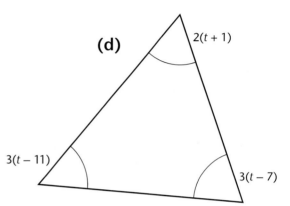
$2(t + 1)$
$3(t - 11)$
$3(t - 7)$

2. Construct and simplify linear equations to help you find these angles.

(a)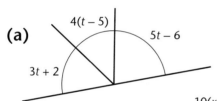
$4(t - 5)$
$5t - 6$
$3t + 2$

(b)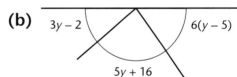
$3y - 2$
$6(y - 5)$
$5y + 16$

(c)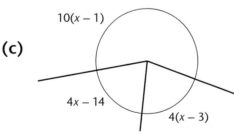
$10(x - 1)$
$4x - 14$
$4(x - 3)$

(d)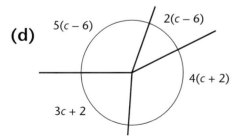
$5(c - 6)$
$2(c - 6)$
$4(c + 2)$
$3c + 2$

(e)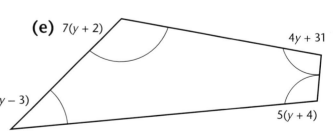
$7(y + 2)$
$4y + 31$
$3(y - 3)$
$5(y + 4)$

NOW TRY THIS!
- Draw a quadrilateral to match each description. Use a protractor.
  (a) This quadrilateral has the angles: $x°$, $2x°$, $3x°$ and $4x°$.
  (b) This quadrilateral has the angles: $y°$, $5y°$, $4y°$ and $2y°$.
  (c) This quadrilateral has the angles: $z°$, $1.5z°$, $2.5z°$ and $3z°$.

 A **linear equation** is one that does not use squared or cubed values. For each question on this page, construct a linear equation using the expressions. Put the expressions equal to 180° or 360°. Remember that the angles inside a triangle total 180°. Angles on a straight line also total 180°. Angles about a point and angles inside a quadrilateral total 360°.

Developing Numeracy
Algebra
Year 9
© A & C BLACK

23

On both sides

A   Amy and Jamie are each following a different instruction.

I multiply by 3 and add 2.   I multiply by 4 and subtract 7.

Starting number	Amy's answer	Jamie's answer
5		
6		
7		

(a) Complete the table.

(b) For which starting number would Amy and Jamie both get the same answer? Use the equation to help you.

$$3x + 2 = 4x - 7$$

 x stands for the starting number.

B Write equations to help you find which starting number gives Amy and Jamie the same answer. Use the letter *x* to stand for the starting number.

(a) 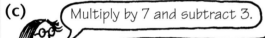 Multiply by 4 and add 2.

Multiply by 2 and add 6.

(b) Multiply by 2 and add 6.

Multiply by 5 and subtract 6.

(c) 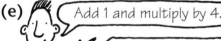 Multiply by 7 and subtract 3.

Multiply by 4 and add 12.

(d) Multiply by 6 and subtract 4.

Multiply by 5 and subtract 2.

(e) Add 1 and multiply by 4.

Multiply by 2 and subtract 4.

(f) Add 3 and multiply by 2.

Multiply by 5 and subtract 6.

(g) Subtract 7 and multiply by 3.

Multiply by 4 and subtract 12.

(h) Subtract 5 and multiply by 4.

Multiply by 10 and subtract 2.

In part B, brackets may be needed: for example, 'subtract 5 and multiply by 4' is 4(*n* − 5). Check your solutions by replacing the letter in the equation with the value you have worked out. Both sides of the equals sign should have the same value. Remember that the value of the letter can be positive or negative.

Developing Numeracy
Algebra
Year 9
© A & C BLACK

On both sides

C

1. The expressions show the length in centimetres of opposite sides of each rectangle. Use them to find the value of the letter x. Give the length of the sides.

The rectangles are not to scale. **!**

(a)

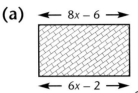

← 8x – 6 →

← 6x – 2 →

$8x - 6 = 6x - 2$
$8x = 6x + 4$
$2x = 4$
$\underline{x = 2}$
So if $x = 2$, $8x - 6$
$= 16 - 6$
$= 10$
Length of side is 10 cm

(b)

← 4x – 12 →

← 6 + 3x →

(c)

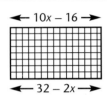

← 10x – 16 →

← 32 – 2x →

(d)

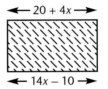

← 20 + 4x →

← 14x – 10 →

(e)

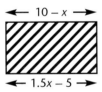

← 10 – x →

← 1.5x – 5 →

(f)

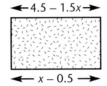

← 4.5 – 1.5x →

← x – 0.5 →

2. The area of each rectangle above is 180 cm². Find the perimeters.

(a) _____ **(b)** _____ **(c)** _____

(d) _____ **(e)** _____ **(f)** _____

NOW TRY THIS!

- Write an equation for this problem and solve it.

A club hired four identical coaches to take its members on a trip. The coaches were filled but still everyone could not fit in. Six people had to go by train. On the return journey, only one coach was available and the remaining 150 people had to get the train.

How many people went on the trip? _____

- Write a similar problem for a partner to solve.

 Check your solutions by replacing the letter in the equation with the value you have worked out. Both sides of the equals sign should have the same value.

Table trials

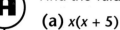

A Find the values of these expressions for different values of *x*. Complete the tables.

(a) $x(x + 5)$

x	*x* + 5	*x*(*x* + 5)
5	10	50
6		
5.6		
5.65		
5.64		
5.63		

(b) $x(11 - x)$

x	11 − *x*	*x*(11 − *x*)
4		
5		
4.5		
4.4		
4.39		
4.38		

(c) $x(x + 0.8)$

x	*x* + 0.8	*x*(*x* + 0.8)
2.7		
2.6		
2.65		
2.64		
2.63		
2.62		

(d) $x(8.6 - x)$

x	8.6 − *x*	*x*(8.6 − *x*)
8		
7.9		
7.95		
7.96		
7.97		
7.98		

(e) $x(x + 19)$

x	*x* + 19	*x*(*x* + 19)
1		
0		
0.5		
0.6		
0.52		
0.51		

(f) $x(9.1 - x)$

x	9.1 − *x*	*x*(9.1 − *x*)
3		
4		
3.7		
3.8		
3.72		
3.71		

B Use the tables above to help you answer these questions. Say between which two decimals (with two decimal places) the solution lies.

(a) $x(x + 5) = 60$ *x* must be between _____ and _____

(b) $x(11 - x) = 29$ *x* must be between _____ and _____

(c) $x(x + 0.8) = 9$ *x* must be between _____ and _____

(d) $x(8.6 - x) = 5$ *x* must be between _____ and _____

(e) $x(x + 19) = 10$ *x* must be between _____ and _____

(f) $x(9.1 - x) = 20$ *x* must be between _____ and _____

 In part B, you are using **trial and improvement** to find a value of *x*. This means testing a solution and using what you find out to pick a closer solution. Take care when you order decimals. Compare the digits in order, starting with the most significant digit (the one furthest to the left).

Table trials

C Each label has an area of approximately 39 cm^2.

$x + 4$

x

$6 + x$
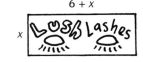
x

$x + 8$

x

$x - 3$

x

Choose different values for x. Use the tables to help you find areas as close as possible to **39**.
Write values for the length and width (to two decimal places).

(a) Area = $x(x + 4)$

x	$x + 4$	$x(x + 4)$	Too large/ small?
4			

Length: _____ cm   Width: _____ cm

(b) Area = $x(6 + x)$

x	$6 + x$	$x(6 + x)$	Too large/ small?
3			

Length: _____ cm   Width: _____ cm

(c) Area = $x(x + 8)$

x	$x + 8$	$x(x + 8)$	Too large/ small?

Length: _____ cm   Width: _____ cm

(d) Area = $x(x - 3)$

x	$x - 3$	$x(x - 3)$	Too large/ small?

Length: _____ cm   Width: _____ cm

NOW TRY THIS!

The product of three consecutive integers is 24 360.

Let n be the first integer, $n + 1$ the second and $n + 2$ the third.

$$n \times (n + 1) \times (n + 2) = 24\,360$$

• Draw a table with the following headings. Use it to find the solution.

n	$n + 1$	$n + 2$	$n \times (n + 1) \times (n + 2)$	Too large/small?

 Always check to see whether the value of the expression is larger or smaller than the value you are aiming for. Use this information to help you choose a larger or smaller value of x for your next calculation. Take care when you order decimals. Compare the digits in order, starting with the most significant digit (the one furthest to the left).

What's the solution?

A

1. Solve these equations. Each equation has two solutions.

(a) $a^2 = 81$ _a = 9 and a = ⁻9_   **(b)** $c^2 + 17 = 53$ _____

(c) $n^2 - 52 = 117$ _____   **(d)** $4m^2 = 100$ _____

(e) $t^2 + 4.7 = 6.39$ _____   **(f)** $(y + 2)^2 = 49$ _y = 5 and y = ⁻9_

(g) $(s + 2)^2 = 16$ _____   **(h)** $(g + 1)^2 = 42.25$ _____

(i) $x - 1 = \dfrac{49}{x - 1}$ _____   **(j)** $\dfrac{36}{p + 4} = p + 4$ _____

(k) $3 = \dfrac{27}{x^2}$ _____   **(l)** $\dfrac{88}{h^2} = 5.5$ _____

2. Solve these equations. Each has only one solution. Give your answers to 1 d.p.

(a) $a^3 = 64$ _a = 4_   **(b)** $c^3 + 17 = 108$ _____

(c) $n^3 - 53 = 565$ _____   **(d)** $2m^3 = 54$ _____

(e) $t^3 - 1.125 = 4.5$ _____   **(f)** $y^3 - 0.088 = 74$ _____

B

1. Find the most accurate value of n (to 2 d.p.), where $n^3 + n = 100$. To do this, write the same integer or decimal (up to 2 d.p.) in both boxes. Use **trial and improvement** to find the answer closest to 100.

Difference between answer and 100

| $\boxed{4}^3$ | $+$ | $\boxed{4}$ | $=$ | 68 | 32 too small |

| $\boxed{5}^3$ | $+$ | $\boxed{5}$ | $=$ | ___ | ___ |

| $\boxed{}^3$ | $+$ | $\boxed{}$ | $=$ | ___ | ___ |

| $\boxed{}^3$ | $+$ | $\boxed{}$ | $=$ | ___ | ___ |

| $\boxed{}^3$ | $+$ | $\boxed{}$ | $=$ | ___ | ___ |

| $\boxed{}^3$ | $+$ | $\boxed{}$ | $=$ | ___ | ___ |

| $\boxed{}^3$ | $+$ | $\boxed{}$ | $=$ | ___ | ___ |

| $\boxed{}^3$ | $+$ | $\boxed{}$ | $=$ | ___ | ___ |

2. This can be written as $n^3 + n = 100$. Give n to 2 d.p. _____

Trial and improvement means testing a solution and using what you find out to pick a closer solution. Take care when you order decimals. Compare the digits in order, starting with the most significant digit (the one furthest to the left).

Developing Numeracy
Algebra
Year 9
© A & C BLACK

What's the solution?

C

1. Use **trial and improvement** to solve these equations. Find an answer to 2 d.p.

(a) $y^3 + y = 80$

$y = 4$ $4^3 + 4 = 68$ *too small*
$y = 5$ $5^3 + 5 = 130$ *too large*
$y = 4.5$

Keep going until you get as close as you can to the answer.

(b) $n^3 - n = 566$

(c) $m^3 = 54 + m$

2. This cuboid has a height of 12.00 cm and a volume of 275.07 cm^3.
The length of the cuboid is 6 cm greater than the width.

width $\times$ length $\times$ height = volume
$y(y + 6) \times 12 = 275.07$

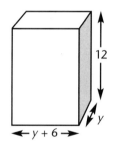

12

y

$\leftarrow y + 6 \rightarrow$

(a) Complete this table to find the width of the cuboid.

y	$y + 6$	$y(y + 6)$	$y(y + 6) \times 12$	Too large/small? (Target: 275.07)
2	8	16	192	*too small*

(b) Give the length and width of the cuboid in centimetres: length _____

width _____

NOW TRY THIS!

• Solve these equations. Draw tables like the one above to help you.

(a) $x(x + 4) \times 8 = 728.5$ **(b)** $c(c - 8) \times 16 = 120.36$ **(c)** $m(10 - m) \times 16 = 339.16$

If you are asked to give an answer to one or two decimal places, this means that there may not be an exact answer, but that your solution should be as close as possible (to 1 or 2 d.p.).

Direct proportion

A If two ⬚variables⬚ are ⬚directly proportional⬚, this means that as one increases in equal amounts, so does the other. A graph of directly proportional values is a straight line that passes through the origin (0, 0).

1. (a) Complete the table to show values of *x* and *y* for the relationship ⬚$y = 4.5x$⬚.

x	1	2	3	4	5	6	7	8	9	10
y	4.5									

(b) Only one person is telling the truth about the values in this table. Tick the true statement.

As *x* increases by equal amounts, *y* decreases by equal amounts. ⬚

As *x* increases by equal amounts, *y* decreases by decreasing amounts. ⬚

As *x* increases by equal amounts, *y* increases by equal amounts. ⬚

2. If this information is used to draw a graph of *y* against *x*, will the line:

(a) be curved? ⬚   **(b)** be straight? ⬚   **(c)** pass through the origin? ⬚

3. For the relationship ⬚$y = 4.5x$⬚, is *y* directly proportional to *x*?   Yes ⬚   No ⬚

B

1. (a) Complete the table to show values of *x* and *y* for the relationship ⬚$y = 25x$⬚.

x	1	2	3	4	5	6	7	8	9	10
y										

(b) Write each set of values of *y* and *x* in the form $\frac{y}{x}$.

$$\frac{y}{x} = \frac{25}{1}, \frac{50}{2},$$ _____

(c) Work out each fraction you have written as a whole number. What do you notice?

_____

(d) Is *y* directly proportional to *x*?   Yes ⬚   No ⬚

2. (a) Tick the relationships below which show *y* directly proportional to *x*.

$y = 3 + x$ ⬚ $y = 4x$ ⬚ $y = \frac{x}{2}$ ⬚ $y = 2x + 1$ ⬚

(b) On squared paper, draw these graphs to check your answers.

If *x* and *y* are **variable**, it means that the value of one letter depends on the value of the other (for example, $y = 2x$). In question B2, draw a table before you draw the graphs of the relationships. Use the table to find the value of *y* for different values of *x*. Then use this to plot pairs of values as coordinates.

Developing Numeracy
Algebra
Year 9
© A & C BLACK

Direct proportion

C

1. (a) Complete the table to show values of x and y for the relationship $\boxed{y = 7.9x}$.

x	1	2	3	4	5	6	7	8	9	10
y										

(b) Write each set of values of y and x in the form $\frac{y}{x}$.

$$\frac{y}{x} = \frac{7.9}{1}, \frac{15.8}{2}, \underline{\hspace{5cm}}$$

(c) What is the value of each fraction? _____

2. Use the information above to help you answer these questions.

(a) Three CDs cost £23.70. How much do seven CDs cost? _____

(b) In a row of identical terraced houses, four house fronts have a total width of 31.6 m. What is the total width of nine houses in this terrace? _____

(c) A 79-cm piece of string is cut into ten equal lengths. What is the total length of six of these pieces? _____

3. Write fractions in a similar form to help you answer these questions.

(a) A scientist mixes 3 parts of dye with 8 parts of water. If she uses 360 ml of water, how much dye does she use?

$$\frac{dye}{water} \qquad \frac{3}{8} = \frac{a}{360}$$

$$a = \underline{\hspace{3cm}}$$

(b) A scientist mixes 7 parts of dye with 5 parts of water. If she uses 545 ml of water, how much dye does she use?

(c) A scientist mixes 6 parts of dye with 7 parts of water. If she makes 494 ml of mixture, how much dye does she use?

$$\frac{dye}{mixture}$$

(d) A scientist mixes 4 parts of dye with 7 parts of water. If she makes 500 ml of mixture, how much dye does she use to the nearest millilitre?

NOW TRY THIS!

- Look carefully at the diagram of this slope. Give the values of a and b.

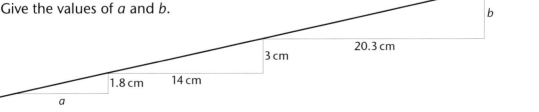

1.8 cm   14 cm   3 cm   20.3 cm b

a

- Suggest horizontal and vertical values for another triangle along this line.

Things are in **direct proportion** when, as one thing increases, so does the other in the same ratio.

Developing Numeracy
Algebra
Year 9
© A & C BLACK

Code-crackers

A

Find the value of each expression for the given value of x.

(a) $x^2 - 5$ if $x = {}^-3$ _____

(b) $(x - 8)^2$ if $x = 5$ _____

(c) $x^2 + 6$ if $x = 0.1$ _____

(d) $x^3 - x$ if $x = 4$ _____

(e) $2x^3$ if $x = {}^-2$ _____

(f) $x^2 + x$ if $x = 5$ _____

(g) $^-x^2$ if $x = {}^-4$ _____

(h) $2x^3$ if $x = {}^-1$ _____

(i) $(5x)^2 - 2x$ if $x = 2$ _____

(j) $6(x^3 + x)$ if $x = 0.1$ _____

B

☆ Substitute the values of a into each equation.

☆ For each answer, use the wheel to find a code letter.

☆ Once you have found the letters for each question, rearrange them to spell a word.

☆ Make a sentence and follow the instruction.

Quick Fix

Record on the back of this sheet.

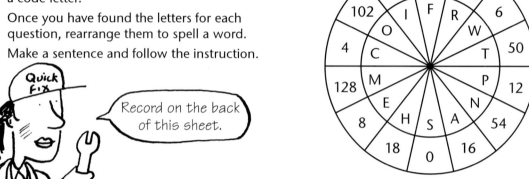

(a) $y = 2(a + 3)$

If $a = 1$, $y =$ _____   If $a = 5$, $y =$ _____

Code letter _____   Code letter _____

If $a = 24$, $y =$ _____   If $a = 61$, $y =$ _____

Code letter _____   Code letter _____

Code word _____

(b) $y = a^2 + 18a - 13$

If $a = 1$, $y =$ _____   If $a = 5$, $y =$ _____   If $a = 3$, $y =$ _____

Code letter _____   Code letter _____   Code letter _____

Code word _____

(c) $y = a(4 + a) - a^2$

If $a = 0$, $y =$ _____   If $a = 1$, $y =$ _____

Code letter _____   Code letter _____

If $a = 4$, $y =$ _____   If $a = 6$, $y =$ _____

Code letter _____   Code letter _____

Code word _____

Remember that the product of two negative numbers is positive, so the square of a negative number is positive. When you rearrange the letters to make the words, try to find three words which make sense as a sentence.

Developing Numeracy
Algebra
Year 9

Code-crackers

☆ Substitute the values of a into each equation.
☆ For each answer, use the wheel to find a code letter.
☆ Once you have found the letters for each question, rearrange them to spell a word.
☆ Make a question and answer it.

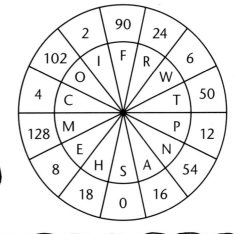

Record on the back of this sheet.

(a) $y = 4a^2 + 2$

If $a = 5$, $y =$ _____   If $a = 1$, $y =$ _____   If $a = 2$, $y =$ _____
Code letter _____   Code letter _____   Code letter _____

(b) $y = 2(a^2 - 1)$

If $a = 3$, $y =$ _____   If $a = 1$, $y =$ _____   If $a = 2$, $y =$ _____
Code letter _____   Code letter _____   Code letter _____

(c) $y = \frac{a^2}{2}$

If $a = 4$, $y =$ _____   If $a = 6$, $y =$ _____   If $a = 10$, $y =$ _____
Code letter _____   Code letter _____   Code letter _____

(d) $y = \frac{a^3 - a^2}{2}$

If $a = 2$, $y =$ _____   If $a = 4$, $y =$ _____   If $a = 6$, $y =$ _____
Code letter _____   Code letter _____   Code letter _____

If $a = 5$, $y =$ _____   If $a = 1$, $y =$ _____
Code letter _____   Code letter _____

(e) $y = 2a^3$

If $a = 2$, $y =$ _____   If $a = 4$, $y =$ _____   If $a = 3$, $y =$ _____
Code letter _____   Code letter _____   Code letter _____

(f) $y = 2(a - 3)^3$

If $a = 6$, $y =$ _____   If $a = 4$, $y =$ _____
Code letter _____   Code letter _____

(g) $y = \frac{4a^3}{a^2}$

If $a = 1$, $y =$ _____   If $a = 2$, $y =$ _____   If $a = 4$, $y =$ _____
Code letter _____   Code letter _____   Code letter _____

If $a = 3$, $y =$ _____   If $a = 0$, $y =$ _____
Code letter _____   Code letter _____

NOW TRY THIS!

• Write expressions using a^3 or a^2 that give the following code letters, when $a = {}^-4$.

(a) P _____   **(b)** E _____   **(c)** N _____

Remember to use the order of BODMAS. In an expression like $3x^2$, square the number before you multiply (for example, if x is 2, the value of the expression is $3 \times 2^2 = 3 \times 4 = 12$). When you rearrange the letters to make the words, try to find seven words which make sense as a question.

Developing Numeracy
Algebra
Year 9
© A & C BLACK

33

A matter of degrees

A

Temperature can be measured in degrees Celsius (°C) or in degrees Fahrenheit (°F). This formula shows the relationship between the two sets of units, where *C* stands for degrees Celsius and *F* for degrees Fahrenheit.

$$F = \frac{9C}{5} + 32$$

1. Convert these temperatures from degrees Celsius to degrees Fahrenheit. Give your answers to the nearest degree.

(a) 5°C   _41°F_   (b) 15°C _____   (c) 20°C _____

(d) 25°C _____   (e) ⁻10°C _____   (f) ⁻30°C _____

(g) 17°C _____   (h) 23°C _____   (i) 32°C _____

(j) 37°C _____   (k) 41°C _____   (l) 44°C _____

(m) ⁻22°C _____   (n) ⁻24°C _____   (o) ⁻28°C _____

The formula above can be rewritten to make *C* the subject of the formula.

$$C = \frac{5}{9}(F - 32)$$

2. Use this new formula to convert these temperatures from degrees Fahrenheit to degrees Celsius. Give your answers to the nearest degree.

(a) 50°F   _10°C_   (b) 95°F _____   (c) 104°F _____

(d) 23°F _____   (e) 5°F _____   (f) ⁻13°F _____

(g) 32°F _____   (h) 47°F _____   (i) 53°F _____

(j) 59°F _____   (k) 64°F _____   (l) 75°F _____

(m) 82°F _____   (n) ⁻20°F _____   (o) ⁻24°F _____

B

One of the following is an alternative formula for converting from degrees Celsius to degrees Fahrenheit. Substitute several of the temperatures in question 1 into each formula to find which one is correct.

$$F = \frac{5C}{9} - 32 \qquad F = \frac{4}{5}(C + 32) \qquad F = \frac{9}{5}(C + 40) - 40$$

_____   _____   _____

_____   _____   _____

_____   _____   _____

Give your answers to the nearest degree by rounding up or down. The formula for converting between Celsius and Fahrenheit temperatures can be expressed in many different ways (for example, where *C* or *F* is the subject of the formula, and with or without brackets).

Developing Numeracy
Algebra
Year 9
© A & C BLACK

A matter of degrees

C Temperature can be measured in degrees Celsius (°C) or in degrees Fahrenheit (°F). This formula shows the relationship between the two sets of units, where C stands for degrees Celsius and F for degrees Fahrenheit.

$$F = \frac{9C}{5} + 32$$

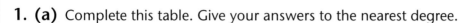

1. (a) Complete this table. Give your answers to the nearest degree.

°C	−50	−35	−30	−10	0	10	20	30
°F								

(b) Give a temperature from the table where the number of degrees Fahrenheit is **more than** the number of degrees Celsius. Write this temperature using both units.

_____ and _____

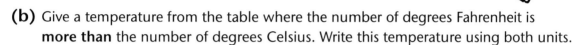

(c) Give a temperature from the table where the number of degrees Fahrenheit is **less than** the number of degrees Celsius. Write this temperature using both units.

_____ and _____

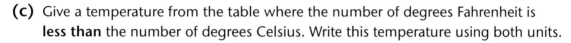

2. (a)

At one temperature there are the same number of degrees Fahrenheit as degrees Celsius (C = F).

Substitute F for C in the formula. Rearrange it to find the value of F.

$$F = \frac{9C}{5} + 32$$

F = _____

(b)

At one temperature the number of degrees Fahrenheit is 20 more than when recorded as degrees Celsius.

Use the formula to find this temperature in degrees Fahrenheit. _____

(c)

At one temperature the number of degrees Fahrenheit is 40 less than when recorded as degrees Celsius.

Use the formula to find this temperature in degrees Fahrenheit. _____

NOW TRY THIS!

• Prove that these two formulae are equivalent by simplifying the second formula.

$$F = \frac{9C}{5} + 32$$

$$F = \frac{9}{5}(C + 40) - 40$$

• Rearrange the first formula to make C the subject.

  To simplify the second formula in the 'Now try this!' challenge, expand the brackets first.

Change the subject

A To change the subject of a formula, use ⊏inverses⊐. Rearrange the formula so that the subject is on its own on one side of the equals sign.

Example: Change $A = BC$ to make B the subject $\longrightarrow$ $B = \dfrac{A}{C}$

Move along the slide and change the subject of each formula. Make the subject of the formula the letter given in the circle.

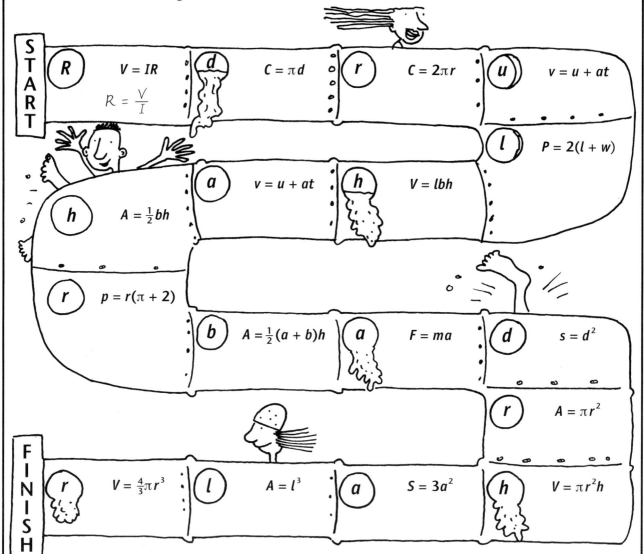

START

R $\quad V = IR \qquad R = \dfrac{V}{I}$

d $\quad C = \pi d$

r $\quad C = 2\pi r$

u $\quad v = u + at$

l $\quad P = 2(l + w)$

a $\quad v = u + at$

h $\quad V = lbh$

h $\quad A = \tfrac{1}{2}bh$

r $\quad p = r(\pi + 2)$

b $\quad A = \tfrac{1}{2}(a + b)h$

a $\quad F = ma$

d $\quad s = d^2$

r $\quad A = \pi r^2$

r $\quad V = \tfrac{4}{3}\pi r^3$

l $\quad A = l^3$

a $\quad S = 3a^2$

h $\quad V = \pi r^2 h$

FINISH

B Which of the original formulae above might you use to find:

(a) the volume of a cuboid?

(b) the perimeter of a rectangle?

(c) the area of a triangle?

(d) the area of a circle?

(e) the volume of a cylinder?

(f) the area of a trapezium?

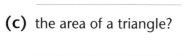

Remember: addition is the **inverse** of subtraction, and vice versa. Multiplication is the inverse of division, and vice versa. There is often more than one way to write a formula: for example, $C = 2ab$ can be rearranged with a as the subject to give the formula $a = \dfrac{c}{2b}$ or $a = \dfrac{1}{2}\dfrac{c}{b}$.

Developing Numeracy
Algebra
Year 9
© A & C BLACK

Change the subject

C

1. The formula for finding the area of an ellipse is $A = \pi ab$.
Make b the subject of the formula.

_____

2. Use your new formula to find the value of b for these ellipses. Give your answers to 1 d.p.

(a) $A = 48\,\text{cm}^2$

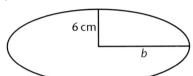

6 cm

b

_____

(b) $A = 64\,\text{cm}^2$

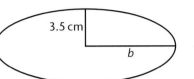

3.5 cm

b

_____

(c) $A = 27\,\text{cm}^2$

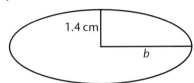

1.4 cm

b

_____

(d) $A = 55\,\text{cm}^2$

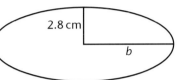

2.8 cm

b

_____

3. The formula for finding the volume of a cylinder is $V = \pi r^2 h$.
Make r the subject of the formula.

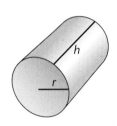

_____

4. Use your new formula to find the value of r for these cylinders.
Give your answers to 1 d.p.

(a) $V = 28\,\text{cm}^3$

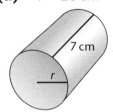

7 cm

r

_____

(b) $V = 36\,\text{cm}^3$

6.5 cm

r

_____

(c) $V = 41\,\text{cm}^3$

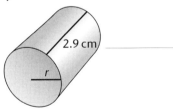

2.9 cm

r

_____

(d) $V = 83\,\text{cm}^3$

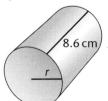

8.6 cm

r

_____

(e) $V = 79\,\text{cm}^3$

7.4 cm

r

_____

(f) $V = 94\,\text{cm}^3$

11.1 cm

r

_____

NOW TRY THIS!

● Change the subject of each formula below.

(a) Make l the subject

$$T = 2\pi\sqrt{\left(\frac{l}{g}\right)}$$

(b) Make w the subject

$$R = \sqrt{\frac{(l + w)}{5}}$$

(c) Make t the subject

$$S = \frac{5}{(t^2 - u)}$$

_____

To change the subject of a formula, use inverses. Rearrange the formula so
that the subject is on its own on one side of the equals sign: for example, if
you change $A = BC$ to make B the subject, the new formula is $B = \frac{A}{C}$.

Developing Numeracy
Algebra
Year 9
© A & C BLACK

Strive to derive

A **1.** Write a formula to match each of the cooking times in this recipe book. Call the number of minutes *m* and the number of kilograms of meat *x*.

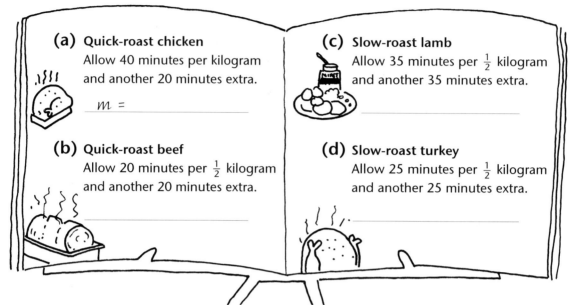

(a) Quick-roast chicken
Allow 40 minutes per kilogram and another 20 minutes extra.

m = _____

(b) Quick-roast beef
Allow 20 minutes per $\frac{1}{2}$ kilogram and another 20 minutes extra.

(c) Slow-roast lamb
Allow 35 minutes per $\frac{1}{2}$ kilogram and another 35 minutes extra.

(d) Slow-roast turkey
Allow 25 minutes per $\frac{1}{2}$ kilogram and another 25 minutes extra.

2. Use your formulae to find the roasting times of these meat dishes. Give each answer in minutes first, then convert this to hours and minutes.

		Minutes	Hours and minutes
(a)	5 kg chicken		
(b)	3.5 kg joint of beef		
(c)	5.5 kg leg of lamb		
(d)	14.2 kg turkey		

B **1.** A mobile phone company charges a connection fee of 8.5p and then charges 9.9p per minute for calls.
Write a formula for the total cost (*c*) in pence of a call lasting *m* minutes. _____

Connection fee   8.5p
Charge per minute 9.9p

2. Write similar formulae to show the costs for these phone companies.

(a)

TALK2
Connection fee   6.2p
Charge per minute   11p

(b)

CHIT CHAT
Connection fee   9.5p
Charge per minute 5.2p

3. Use your formulae to find which company would charge the least for:

(a) 1 minute   **(b)** 5 minutes   **(c)** 15 minutes

Formulae which use letters to stand for numbers are useful because you can substitute any numbers you choose.

Strive to derive

C Chloe timed a ball rolling down slopes of different lengths.
She set the angle of the slope to be the same throughout.

Here are some of her results.

Length of slope (L) in metres	$\frac{1}{2}$	2	8	18	32	50	200
Time (T) taken for a ball to roll down in seconds	1	2	4	6	8	10	20

1. Chloe discovered a relationship between the length (L) and the time (T), which can be written as a formula.

(a) To find this formula, first work out the values of T^2. Complete the table.

Length of slope (L) in metres	$\frac{1}{2}$	2	8	18	32	50	200
Time (T) taken for a ball to roll down in seconds	1	2	4	6	8	10	20
T^2							

(b) Look for a relationship between the values of T^2 and L. Write a formula to show the relationship between T and L. _____

2. Chloe changed the angle of the slope. Here are her results, with the times given to 1 d.p.

(a) Find the approximate values of T^2, to the nearest whole number.

Length of slope (L) in metres	$\frac{1}{2}$	2	8	18	32	50	200
Time (T) taken for a ball to roll down in seconds	1.4	2.8	5.7	8.5	11.3	14.1	28.3
T^2							

(b) Look for a relationship between the values of T^2 and L for this slope. Write a formula to show the relationship between T and L. _____

NOW TRY THIS!

This is the formula for a slope at a different angle. It shows T in terms of L.

$$T = \sqrt{(2L \div 3)}$$

● Find the time (T), to the nearest second, a ball would take to roll down a slope 32 m long. _____

  Formulae which use letters to stand for numbers are useful because you can substitute any numbers you choose.

The generation game

A Write the | position-to-term rule | as simply as you can. Use the letter *n* to stand for the position number in the sequence. Then generate the first six terms.

(a) Multiply the position number by 5 and subtract this from 20.

$20 - 5n$

Position (*n*)	1	2	3	4	5	6 ...
Term	15,	10,	5,	0,	⁻5,	⁻10...

(b) Multiply the position number by 4 and subtract this from 22.

Position (*n*)	1	2	3	4	5	6 ...
Term						

(c) Multiply the position number by 3 and add 2.

Position (*n*)	1	2	3	4	5	6 ...
Term						

(d) Multiply the position number by 4 and subtract 1.

Position (*n*)	1	2	3	4	5	6 ...
Term						

(e) Multiply the position number by 6 and subtract 3.

Position (*n*)	1	2	3	4	5	6 ...
Term						

(f) Multiply the position number by 7 and subtract this from 19.

Position (*n*)	1	2	3	4	5	6 ...
Term						

(g) Add 4 to the position number and multiply by 4.

Position (*n*)	1	2	3	4	5	6 ...
Term						

(h) Subtract 5 from the position number and multiply by 3.

Position (*n*)	1	2	3	4	5	6 ...
Term						

B Use the rules which contain the letter *n* to find the 10th, 20th and 100th term of each sequence above.

Sequence	(a)	(b)	(c)	(d)	(e)	(f)	(g)	(h)
10th term								
20th term								
100th term								

The **position-to-term rule** tells you how each number in the sequence relates to the position number. The letter *n* is often used to stand for the position number. Sequences that have a rule where *n* is subtracted from a number (for example, 20 – 5*n* or 22 – 4*n*) are **descending** sequences, where each term is smaller than the previous term.

Developing Numeracy
Algebra
Year 9
© A & C BLACK

The generation game

C

1. Generate a sequence that fits each description. Write the first six terms.

(a) Every other number in the sequence is an integer.

2, 2.5, 3, 3.5, 4, 4.5

(b) All the numbers in the sequence are multiples of 6.

(c) No number in the sequence is an integer.

(d) No odd numbers appear in the sequence.

(e) Every other number in the sequence ends with the digit 8.

(f) The terms of the sequence decrease in size.

(g) No terms are multiples of 3, but the difference between terms is 3.

(h) The first term is ⁻46. Every other number is an integer.

(i) No terms are multiples of 7, but the difference between terms is 7.

(j) Every fourth number in the sequence is an integer.

(k) There is only one single-digit number in the sequence.

(l) The fifth term of the sequence is 0.4.

(m) There are exactly 10 two-digit numbers in the sequence.

(n) The hundredth term of the sequence is 98.

(o) The hundredth term of the sequence is 407.

2. How many of your sequences are:

(a) ascending? _____ **(b) descending?** _____

3. Compare each of your sequences with a partner.

Are any different?

NOW TRY THIS!

- Write the **position-to-term rule** for each sequence above. Use the letter *n* to stand for the position number.

In **ascending** sequences, each term is larger than the previous term. In **descending** sequences, each term is smaller than the previous term. The **position-to-term rule** tells you how each number in the sequence relates to the position number (*n*). The first term in the sequence $3n + 1$ can be found by substituting 1 for *n*, the second term by substituting 2 for *n*, and so on.

The value of a and b

A Compare the rule on each card with the general rule $\boxed{T(n) = an + b}$.
Give the values of a and b. Fill in the table.

Write the first term of the sequence and the difference between adjacent terms.

> $T(n)$ stands for the nth term of the sequence.

(a) $T(n) = 2n + 3$

$a = \underline{\hspace{1cm}}$

$b = \underline{\hspace{1cm}}$

n	1	2	3	4	5	6
$2n + 3$	5	7	9	11	13	15

First term $\underline{\hspace{1cm}}$

Difference between adjacent terms $\underline{\hspace{1cm}}$

(b) $T(n) = 6n + 5$

$a = \underline{\hspace{1cm}}$

$b = \underline{\hspace{1cm}}$

First term $\underline{\hspace{1cm}}$

Difference between adjacent terms $\underline{\hspace{1cm}}$

(c) $T(n) = 2n - 7$

$a = \underline{\hspace{1cm}}$

$b = \underline{\hspace{1cm}}$

First term $\underline{\hspace{1cm}}$

Difference between adjacent terms $\underline{\hspace{1cm}}$

(d) $T(n) = 8 + 5n$

$a = \underline{\hspace{1cm}}$

$b = \underline{\hspace{1cm}}$

First term $\underline{\hspace{1cm}}$

Difference between adjacent terms $\underline{\hspace{1cm}}$

(e) $T(n) = \frac{1}{2}n - 1.5$

$a = \underline{\hspace{1cm}}$

$b = \underline{\hspace{1cm}}$

First term $\underline{\hspace{1cm}}$

Difference between adjacent terms $\underline{\hspace{1cm}}$

B Write what you notice about the first term and the difference. Describe them in terms of a and b. $\underline{\hspace{4cm}}$

$\underline{\hspace{10cm}}$

The values of a and b can be positive or negative. To find the value of a, look at the rule for the sequence and ask: *How many ns are there?* In the sequence $10 - 4n$, $a = {}^-4$; in the sequence $6n - 2$, $a = 6$. To find the value of b, ask: *What number is added or subtracted to the ns?* In the sequence $10 - 4n$, $b = 10$; in the sequence $6n - 2$, $b = {}^-2$.

Developing Numeracy
Algebra
Year 9
© A & C BLACK

The value of a and b

C

1. **(a)** Compare the rule on the card with the general rule $\boxed{T(n) = an + b}$. Complete the card.

$T(n)$ stands for the nth term of the sequence.

$T(n) = 5n - 3$	n	1	2	3	4	5	6
$a = \rule{2em}{0.4pt}$	$5n - 3$						
$b = \rule{2em}{0.4pt}$							

First term _____

Difference between adjacent terms _____

(b) Tick the true statements.

The first term is equal to $a + b$. ☐   The first term is equal to $b - a$. ☐

The difference between adjacent terms is the same as b. ☐

The difference between adjacent terms is the same as a. ☐

2. Play this game with a partner. You need one counter and a dice.

> ☆ Take turns to choose a digit from 1 to 8. Carry on until you each have four different digits.
> ☆ Roll the dice and move the counter. On a separate piece of paper, record the rule you land on. Write the first six terms of its sequence.
> ☆ Each player scores a point for every one of their digits that appears in the sequence: for example, in the sequence 7, 5, 3, 1, ⁻1, ⁻3... score 2 points for the digit 1, if that is your digit, score 2 points for the digit 3, if that is your digit, score 1 point for the digit 5, and so on.
> ☆ The winner is the first player to reach 20 points.

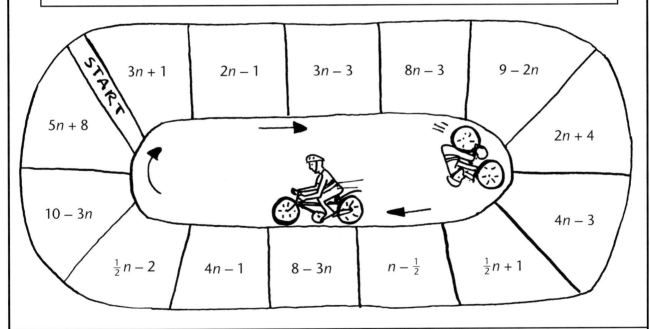

START

$3n + 1$ $2n - 1$ $3n - 3$ $8n - 3$ $9 - 2n$

$5n + 8$ $2n + 4$

$10 - 3n$ $4n - 3$

$\frac{1}{2}n - 2$ $4n - 1$ $8 - 3n$ $n - \frac{1}{2}$ $\frac{1}{2}n + 1$

NOW TRY THIS!

- Which of the rules on the board above:

    (a) does not have any integers in its sequence? _____

    (b) will only ever produce even numbers? _____

The values of a and b can be positive or negative. To find the value of a, look at the rule for the sequence and ask: *How many ns are there?* In the sequence $10 - 4n$, $a = {}^-4$; in the sequence $6n - 2$, $a = 6$. To find the value of b, ask: *What number is added or subtracted to the ns?* In the sequence $10 - 4n$, $b = 10$; in the sequence $6n - 2$, $b = {}^-2$.

Watch the difference!

A

Read these statements and talk to a partner about them.

> Sequences that have a constant difference between adjacent terms (called **linear sequences**) are expressed using the letter n, for example $3n + 4$, $10 - 5n$.
>
> Some sequences where adjacent terms do **not** have a constant difference can be expressed using n^2, for example $4n^2$, $5n^2 - 4$, $6n^2 - n$.

1. Draw arrows to match each rule with the correct sequence. Find the differences between adjacent terms and use the statements above to help you.

(a) 5, 11, 21, 35, 53, 75... $\quad$ 6 10 14 18 22 $\qquad$ $5n + 3$ $\quad$ $2n^2 + 3$ $\qquad$ 8, 13, 18, 23, 28, 33... $\quad$ 5 5 5 5 5

(b) 6, 18, 38, 66, 102... $\qquad$ $4n + 2$ $\quad$ $4n^2 + 2$ $\qquad$ 6, 10, 14, 18, 22, 26...

(c) 2, 7, 12, 17, 22, 27... $\qquad$ $3n^2 - 1$ $\quad$ $5n - 3$ $\qquad$ 2, 11, 26, 47, 74...

(d) 0, 2, 6, 12, 20, 30... $\qquad$ $2(n - 1)$ $\quad$ $n^2 - n$ $\qquad$ 0, 2, 4, 6, 8, 10, 12...

(e) ⁻4, 14, 44, 86, 140... $\qquad$ $6n^2 - 10$ $\quad$ $4n - 8$ $\qquad$ ⁻4, 0, 4, 8, 12, 16...

2. Look at each sequence above whose rule contains n^2. Talk to a partner about any patterns you can see in the row of differences you have written.

B

Write the first six terms of each sequence below.

> $T(n)$ stands for the nth term of the sequence.

(a) $T(n) = n^2$

n	1	2	3	4	5	6
n^2						

(b) $T(n) = n^2 + 3$

n	1	2	3	4	5	6
$n^2 + 3$						

(c) $T(n) = n^2 - 2$

n	1	2	3	4	5	6

(d) $T(n) = 2n^2$

n	1	2	3	4	5	6

(e) $T(n) = 2n^2 + 2$

n	1	2	3	4	5	6

(f) $T(n) = 2n^2 - 3$

n	1	2	3	4	5	6

A **linear sequence** is one that does not use squared or cubed values. It has a constant difference between terms. The sequences on this page which do *not* have a constant difference between terms are expressed using n^2. Other sequences of the same kind could be expressed using n^3 (and others cannot be expressed at all if they do not follow any regular pattern).

Developing Numeracy
Algebra
Year 9
© A & C BLACK

1. For each rule, find the first difference by comparing adjacent terms. Then find the second difference by comparing the numbers in the first difference.

(a) $T(n) = n^2$

n	1	2	3	4	5	6
n^2	1	4	9	16	25	36

3   5   7   9   11   First difference

2   2   2   2   Second difference

(b) $T(n) = 2n^2$

n	1	2	3	4	5	6
$2n^2$						

First difference

Second difference

(c) $T(n) = 3n^2$

n	1	2	3	4	5	6
$3n^2$						

First difference

Second difference

(d) $T(n) = 4n^2$

n	1	2	3	4	5	6
$4n^2$						

First difference

Second difference

(e) $T(n) = 4n^2 + 1$

n	1	2	3	4	5	6
$4n^2 + 1$						

First difference

Second difference

2. Compare each rule with the second difference. What do you notice? _____

_____

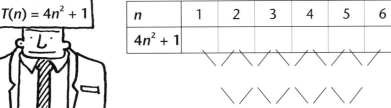

NOW TRY THIS!

● Compare these sequences with the rules above. Write the rule for each.

(a) 4, 13, 28, 49, 76, 109... _____

(b) 6, 18, 38, 66, 102, 146... _____

(c) ⁻1, 2, 7, 14, 23, 34... _____

(d) 12, 18, 28, 42, 60, 82... _____

Remember: $T(n)$ stands for the nth term of a sequence. Sequences involving n^2 are called **quadratic sequences**. They always have a constant second difference. To find the rule of a quadratic sequence, find the first and second differences, then use this to work out how many n^2 are in the rule.

Pattern spotting

A 1. Count the number of squares in each shape.

Complete the table.

Shape number (n)	1	2	3	4	5	6
Number of grey squares	1					
Number of white squares	2					
Total number of squares	3					

2. Describe the patterns you notice for:

   (a) the number of white squares _____

   (b) the number of grey squares _____

   (c) the total number of squares _____

3. How many:

   (a) grey squares will there be in the 100th shape T(100)? _____

   (b) white squares will there be in the 100th shape T(100)? _____

4. Write the **position-to-term rule** for the total number of squares T(n). _____

B 1. Count the number of squares in each shape.

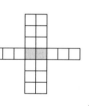

Complete the table.

Shape number (n)	1	2	3	4	5	6
Number of grey squares	2					
Number of white squares	6					
Total number of squares	8					

2. Describe the patterns you notice for:

   (a) the number of white squares _____

   (b) the number of grey squares _____

   (c) the total number of squares _____

3. How many:

   (a) grey squares will there be in the 100th shape T(100)? _____

   (b) white squares will there be in the 100th shape T(100)? _____

4. Write the position-to-term rule for the total number of squares T(n). _____

 The **position-to-term rule** tells you how each number in the sequence relates to the position number. The letter n is often used to stand for the position number. T(n) stands for the nth term of a sequence. T(100) stands for the hundredth term of a sequence. It can be found by substituting 100 for n (for example, in the sequence 3n + 1, T(100) = 301).

Developing Numeracy
Algebra
Year 9
© A & C BLACK

Pattern spotting

1. (a) Count the number of squares in each shape.

Complete the table.

Shape number	1	2	3	4	5	6
Number of squares	1					

First difference

Second difference

(b) Write the **position-to-term rule** for the total number of squares $T(n)$. _____

2. (a) Count the number of squares in each shape.

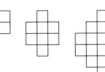 

Complete the table.

Shape number	1	2	3	4	5	6
Number of squares	2					

First difference

Second difference

(b) Write the position-to-term rule for the total number of squares $T(n)$. _____

3. Write a position-to-term rule for this sequence. Explain your reasoning.

   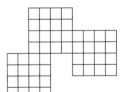

_____

_____

NOW TRY THIS!

- Investigate how many handshakes would occur if each person in a room shook hands once with every other person.

Number of people	1	2	3	4	5	6
Number of handshakes	0	1				

- What is this sequence of numbers called? _____

- Use the first and second differences to find the rule of the sequence.

 The **position-to-term rule** tells you how each number in the sequence relates to the position number. The letter *n* is often used to stand for the position number. $T(n)$ stands for the *n*th term of a sequence. For the 'Now try this!' challenge, remember that when two people shake hands this counts as only one, not two, handshakes.

Shape up

A Count the number of small squares in each shape (include both grey and white squares in your total). Write this as a sequence. Find the **position-to-term rule** for the *n*th term of the sequence.

(a)

3 , _____ *n*th term: _____

(b)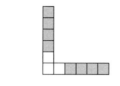

_____ *n*th term: _____

(c)

_____ *n*th term: _____

(d)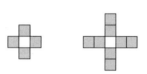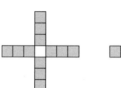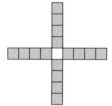

_____ *n*th term: _____

(e)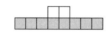

_____ *n*th term: _____

B

1. On squared paper, draw and shade shapes to match each sequence below. Use the given shape as the first term each time.

(a) 6, 9, 12, 15, 18, 21...   **(b)** 6, 10, 14, 18, 22, 26...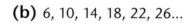

(c) 6, 8, 10, 12, 14, 16...   **(d)** 8, 11, 14, 17, 20, 23...

(e) 7, 11, 15, 19, 23, 27...   **(f)** 5, 8, 11, 14, 17, 20...

2. Now write the position-to-term rule for each of these sequences.

(a) _____   **(b)** _____   **(c)** _____

(d) _____   **(e)** _____   **(f)** _____

The **position-to-term rule** tells you how each number in the sequence relates to the position number. The letter *n* is often used to stand for the position number.

Developing Numeracy
Algebra
Year 9
© A & C BLACK

Shape up

1. (a) In these diagrams, different numbers of circles are placed over each other. Mark the points where the circumferences of the circles touch.

 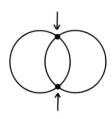 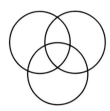 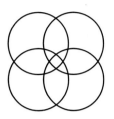 

(b) Fill in the table. Continue the sequence up to the ninth term.

Number of circles	1	2	3	4	5	6	7	8	9
Number of points	0	2							

First difference   2

Second difference

(c) Talk to a partner about the patterns you notice in the number of overlap points.

(d) Prove that the **position-to-term rule** for this sequence is $n^2 - n$. Substitute different values for n into the rule. $1^2 - 1 = 0,\ 2^2 - 2 =$ _____

2. (a) For each shape, join each dot to every other dot.

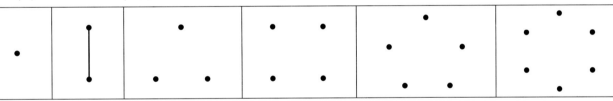

(b) Fill in the table. Continue the sequence up to the ninth term.

Number of dots	1	2	3	4	5	6	7	8	9
Number of lines	0	1							

First difference   1

Second difference

(c) Talk to a partner about the patterns you notice in the number of lines.

(d) Prove that the position-to-term rule for this sequence is $\frac{1}{2}(n^2 - n)$. Substitute different values for n into the rule. _____

NOW TRY THIS!

• Compare the two sequences above. What do you notice? _____

_____

• Make up two other sequences which have a similar relationship.

 The **position-to-term rule** tells you how each number in the sequence relates to the position number. The letter n is often used to stand for the position number.

Developing Numeracy
Algebra
Year 9
© A & C BLACK

49

What's my function?

1. Complete the tables and as many mappings as possible for the following functions.

(a) $x \longrightarrow 2x + 1$

x	0	1	2	3	4	5
$2x + 1$	1					

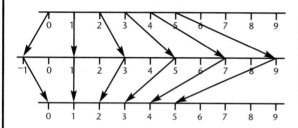

(b) $x \longrightarrow 3x - 2$

x	0	1	2	3	4	5
$3x - 2$						

2. This mapping diagram shows two functions, performed one after the other.

$x \longrightarrow 2x - 1$

$x \longrightarrow \dfrac{(x + 1)}{2}$

(a) What do you notice about the first inputs and final outputs of these functions?

_____

_____

We say $x \longrightarrow \dfrac{(x + 1)}{2}$ is the **inverse** of $x \longrightarrow 2x - 1$.

(b) Complete this table for the function $x \longrightarrow 3x - 1$. Draw arrows on the first part of the mapping diagram.

x	0	1	2	3	4	5
$3x - 1$						

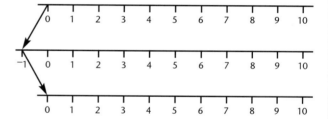

(c) Now draw arrows to take the outputs back to the original inputs.

(d) Write the function which will take the outputs of the function $x \longrightarrow 3x - 1$ back to the original inputs. This is called the inverse function .

1. Write the inverses of these functions.

(a) $x \longrightarrow 2x + 1$ $x \longrightarrow \dfrac{(x - 1)}{2}$

(b) $x \longrightarrow 3x - 2$

(c) $x \longrightarrow \frac{1}{2}x - 5$

(d) $x \longrightarrow 6(4 + x)$

(e) $x \longrightarrow 8x + 4$

(f) $x \longrightarrow 7x - 3$

2. Draw two-tiered mapping diagrams (like those above) to check your inverse functions.

 Remember: addition is the **inverse** of subtraction, and vice versa. Multiplication is the inverse of division, and vice versa. To check your inverses in part B, first draw a table and a mapping diagram for the original function. Then add another tier to the diagram. Check that, for each output value, the inverse function takes it back to the original input.

Developing Numeracy
Algebra
Year 9
© A & C BLACK

What's my function?

C

1. This mapping diagram shows two functions, performed one after the other.

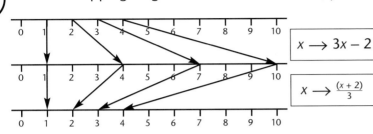

$x \longrightarrow 3x - 2$

$x \longrightarrow \frac{(x + 2)}{3}$

What do you notice about the first inputs and final outputs of these functions?

_____

_____

We say $x \longrightarrow \frac{(x + 2)}{3}$ is the **inverse** of $x \longrightarrow 3x - 2$.

2. (a) Complete this mapping diagram.

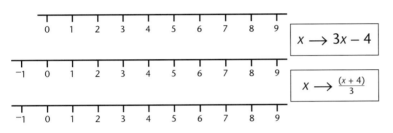

$x \longrightarrow 3x - 4$

$x \longrightarrow \frac{(x + 4)}{3}$

(b) Are these inverses?

Yes ☐   No ☐

3. (a) Complete this mapping diagram.

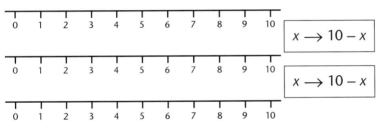

$x \longrightarrow 10 - x$

$x \longrightarrow 10 - x$

(b) Are these inverses?

Yes ☐   No ☐

(c) A function with an inverse which is the same as itself is called a ⟨self-inverse function⟩.
Are these self-inverse functions?   Yes ☐   No ☐

4. Give the inverses of these functions. Draw mappings of each.

(a) $x \longrightarrow 7 - x$ ☐   **(b)** $x \longrightarrow 5 - 2x$ ☐

(c) $x \longrightarrow \frac{1}{4}x + 5$ ☐   **(d)** $x \longrightarrow \frac{1}{2}(x - 2)$ ☐

(e) $x \longrightarrow 3(4 - x)$ ☐   **(f)** $x \longrightarrow \frac{(x + 4)}{3}$ ☐

(g) $x \longrightarrow \frac{(2x - 6)}{10}$ ☐   **(h)** Check your inverse functions using different values of x.

NOW TRY THIS!

• Which of the functions in question 4 are self-inverse functions?

_____

Remember: addition is the **inverse** of subtraction, and vice versa. Multiplication is the inverse of division, and vice versa. To check your inverses in question 4, first draw a table and a mapping diagram for the original function. Then add another tier to the diagram. Check that, for each output value, the inverse function takes it back to the original input.

The plot thickens

A

1. Each function in the first row has been rearranged to make y the subject of the function. Draw lines to join equivalent functions.

| $y + 2x - 1 = 0$ | $y - x + 2 = 0$ | $y - 2x + 1 = 0$ | $y + 2x - 2 = 0$ | $y - x - 1 = 0$ |

| $y = 2x - 1$ | $y = 1 - 2x$ | $y = 2 - 2x$ | $y = x - 2$ | $y = x + 1$ |

2. Rearrange these functions to make y the subject of the function.

(a) $y + 3x - 5 = 0$ $y =$ **(b)** $y - 4x - 6 = 0$ $y =$

(c) $y - 2x + 4 = 0$ $y =$ **(d)** $y + 6x + 2 = 0$ $y =$

(e) $y - 5x - 1 = 0$ $y =$ **(f)** $y + 8x - 9 = 0$ $y =$

B

1. **(a)** Rearrange $y + 2x - 5 = 0$ to make y the subject of the function. _____

(b) Complete the table for this function.

x	-3	-2	-1	0	1	2	3
$y =$							

2. **(a)** Now plot these points on the grid. Join them with a line. Label the line.

(b) At what point does this line cross the y-axis?

(0, ___)

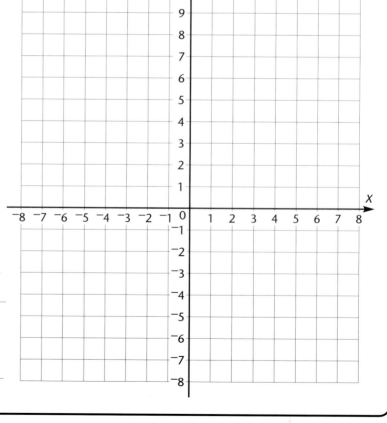

3. Compare your rearranged function above with the general form $y = mx + c$.

(a) What is the value of c? _____

(b) What is the value of m? _____

4. Does your graph slope up to the right or left? _____

 To make y the subject, use inverses to rearrange the expression so that y is on its own on one side of the equals sign. If a point on the grid cannot be joined to the others with a straight line, check your working.

Developing Numeracy
Algebra
Year 9
© A & C BLACK

The plot thickens

C

1. Rearrange these functions to make y the subject of the function.

(a) $\boxed{\frac{y}{3} - x = 0}$ $\boxed{y = 3x}$ **(b)** $\boxed{\frac{y}{4} - x = 0}$ $\boxed{y =}$

(c) $\boxed{\frac{y}{5} + x = 0}$ $\boxed{y =}$ **(d)** $\boxed{y - 7x + 3 = 0}$ $\boxed{y =}$

(e) $\boxed{y - 4x - 5 = 0}$ $\boxed{y =}$ **(f)** $\boxed{y + 7x - 2 = 0}$ $\boxed{y =}$

(g) $\boxed{2y - x = 13}$ $\boxed{y = \frac{(13 + x)}{2}}$ **(h)** $\boxed{2y + 3x = 8}$ $\boxed{y =}$

(i) $\boxed{2y - x + 6 = 0}$ $\boxed{y =}$ **(j)** $\boxed{4y + 5x - 2 = 0}$ $\boxed{y =}$

(k) $\boxed{3y + 2x = {}^-5}$ $\boxed{y =}$ **(l)** $\boxed{5y - 3 = 4x}$ $\boxed{y =}$

2.
Work with a partner. Use a graphical calculator to plot and compare graphs of your
rearranged functions above.

Talk about: the intercept of the y-axis
the direction of the slope
the steepness of the slope.

3. Without plotting a function on a graph, how can you tell:

(a) the intercept of the y-axis? _____

(b) the direction of the slope? _____

(c) the steepness of the slope? _____

NOW TRY THIS!

● For each of these functions, write a description of the graph of the function. Think about
the intercept of the y-axis, the direction of the slope and the steepness of the slope.

$\boxed{y = 4x}$ $\boxed{y = 4x + 3}$ $\boxed{y = \frac{1}{4}x}$

$\boxed{y = {}^-4x}$ $\boxed{y = 5 - 4x}$ $\boxed{y = 4x - 2}$

$\boxed{y + 4x - 1 = 0}$ $\boxed{y = {}^-4x - 3}$ $\boxed{y - 4x = 2}$

$\boxed{\text{Do not draw the graphs.}}$ **!**

To make y the subject, use inverses to rearrange the expression so that y is
on its own on one side of the equals sign.

Find gradients
of linear graphs
(y = mx + c)

Find the gradient

To find the **gradient** of a line, you can draw
horizontal and vertical lines beneath the line
of the graph to form triangles. Find the
lengths of the lines, then divide the vertical
length (*y*) by the horizontal length (*x*).

Gradient = $\frac{\text{change in } y}{\text{change in } x}$

Example: Gradient = $\frac{2}{1}$ = $\frac{4}{2}$ = 2

! Draw at least
two triangles
to check your
gradient.

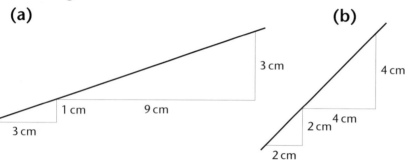

4 cm

2 cm
2 cm

1 cm

Find the gradients of lines with these measurements.

(a)

3 cm

1 cm   9 cm

3 cm

(b)

3 cm

4 cm

2 cm
4 cm

2 cm

(c)

6 cm

2 cm

3 cm

1 cm

Gradient = _____   Gradient = _____   Gradient = _____

B

1. Write these functions. Substitute the given values for the letters *m* and *c* into the
general equation | *y = mx + c* |.

(a) *m* = 2 and *c* = ⁻3 | *y = 2x – 3* | **(b)** *m* = 3 and *c* = 4 | _____ |

(c) *m* = 4 and *c* = ⁻1 | _____ | **(d)** *m* = 5 and *c* = 2 | _____ |

2. For each function above, complete a table of values for *x* and *y*.

(a) *y = 2x – 3*

x	⁻3	⁻2	⁻1	0	1	2	3
y	⁻9						

(b) _____

x	⁻3	⁻2	⁻1	0	1	2	3
y							

(c) _____

x	⁻3	⁻2	⁻1	0	1	2	3
y							

(d) _____

x	⁻3	⁻2	⁻1	0	1	2	3
y							

3. Draw a grid on squared paper and label the axes ⁻20 to 20. For each function above,
plot the points and join them to make a line. Label each line.

4. Draw triangles beneath the lines of the graph like those in part A. Find the lengths of the
vertical and horizontal lines. Work out the gradients.

Gradients: (a) _____ **(b)** _____ **(c)** _____ **(d)** _____

The word **gradient** describes the steepness and slope of a line. Positive
gradients slope up to the right. A line with a gradient of 1 is at 45 degrees
to the horizontal. A line with a gradient between 0 and 1 is between the
horizontal and 45 degree lines. A line with a gradient greater than 1 is
between the 45 degree line and the vertical.

Developing Numeracy
Algebra
Year 9
© A & C BLACK

Find the gradient

1. Write these functions. Substitute the given values for the letters m and c into the general equation $\boxed{y = mx + c}$.

(a) $m = 1$ and $c = 0$ $\boxed{y = x}$ **(b)** $m = 2$ and $c = {}^{-}3$ $\boxed{y = 2x - 3}$

(c) $m = {}^{-}1$ and $c = 0$ $\boxed{}$ **(d)** $m = {}^{-}2$ and $c = 3$ $\boxed{}$

(e) $m = {}^{-}4$ and $c = 2$ $\boxed{}$ **(f)** $m = {}^{-}6$ and $c = {}^{-}2$ $\boxed{}$

2. For each function above, complete a table of values for x and y.

(a) $y = x$

x	$^-3$	$^-2$	$^-1$	0	1	2	3
y	$^-3$	$^-2$	$^-1$				

(b) $y = 2x - 3$

x	$^-3$	$^-2$	$^-1$	0	1	2	3
y							

(c) _____

x	$^-3$	$^-2$	$^-1$	0	1	2	3
y							

(d) _____

x	$^-3$	$^-2$	$^-1$	0	1	2	3
y							

(e) _____

x	$^-3$	$^-2$	$^-1$	0	1	2	3
y							

(f) _____

x	$^-3$	$^-2$	$^-1$	0	1	2	3
y							

3. Draw a grid on squared paper and label the axes $^-20$ to 20. For each function above, plot the points and join them to make a line. Label each line.

4. Draw triangles to help you find the **gradient** of each line. Divide the change in y by the change in x.

$$\text{Gradient} = \frac{\text{change in } y}{\text{change in } x}$$

Gradients: **(a)** ____ **(b)** ____ **(c)** ____

            (d) ____ **(e)** ____ **(f)** ____

NOW TRY THIS!

- Compare the gradients above with the value of m in the function.
- Use what you notice to find which function in each pair below has the steeper gradient. Tick the correct answer.

(a) $\boxed{y = 3x + 9 \;\square}$ $\boxed{y = 4x - 2 \;\square}$ **(b)** $\boxed{y = {}^-3x + 7 \;\square}$ $\boxed{y = {}^-x + 11 \;\square}$

The word **gradient** describes the steepness and slope of a line. In the 'Now try this!' challenge, do *not* draw the graphs of the functions. Work out each gradient by looking at the value of m.

An eye for detail

A

1. Water runs steadily into these containers. The line graphs show the depth of water against time. Match each container with the correct graph.

> Think about whether the depth of the water increases quickly at first, slowly at first, or steadily throughout.

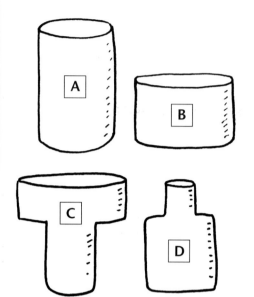

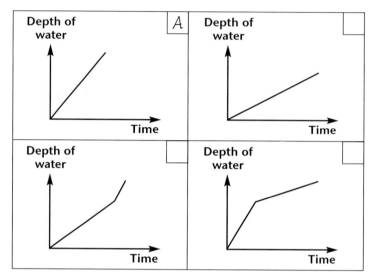

2. Water runs steadily into these containers. Sketch line graphs to show the depth of water against time.

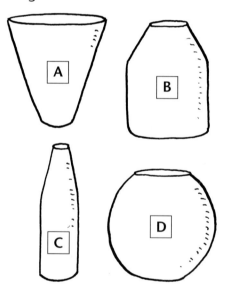

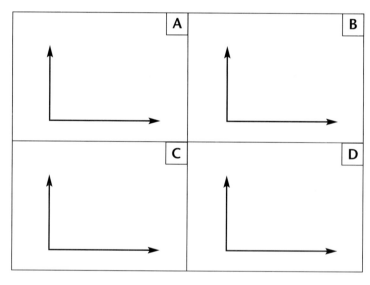

B

Draw containers to match these line graphs.

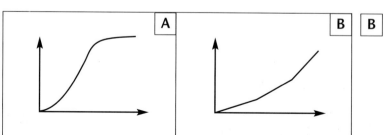

Think carefully about how quickly each container will fill with water. The more quickly it fills, the steeper the slope of the graph will be.

**Developing Numeracy
Algebra
Year 9
© A & C BLACK**

An eye for detail

Plot graphs of
linear functions in
real-life situations

C

1. The wheel of the London Eye turns clockwise at
   a steady rate. Some people get into a carriage.
   The wheel turns through one complete revolution,
   then the people get out.

   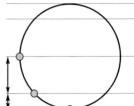

   (a) Draw dots on the remaining circles below, to show
   where the carriage will be at regular time intervals.

   ○ ○ ○ ○ ○ ○ ○ ○ ○

   (b) Use this to help you sketch a line graph. Show the height
   of the carriage above ground level, against time. Notice
   that the height does not increase at a steady rate (for
   instance, it increases slowly at first, then more quickly).

Height

Time

2. Sketch line graphs to match each of the following descriptions.

   (a) When x is small, y is large.
   When x is large, y is small.
   As x increases by equal
   amounts, y decreases
   by equal amounts.

   (b) When x is small, y is small.
   When x is large, y is large.
   As x increases by equal
   amounts, y increases
   by increasing amounts.

   (c) When x is small, y is large.
   When x is large, y is small.
   As x increases by equal
   amounts, y decreases
   by decreasing amounts.

   (d) When x is small, y becomes zero.
   When x is large, y is large.
   As x increases by equal
   amounts, y increases
   by decreasing amounts.

NOW TRY THIS!

Deepak throws three stones at three different angles.

● Draw a distance–time graph. Sketch a line for each stone
  to show the height of the stones against time.

Although the London Eye travels around its centre at a constant rate, the
increase or decrease in **vertical** height over time will not be constant. The
height of the carriage increases slowly at first, as it travels only a small
distance vertically in the first time period.

Developing Numeracy
Algebra
Year 9
© A & C BLACK

Explain that!

A Each card shows a graph with a title. With a partner, write a detailed explanation for the shape of each graph.

(a)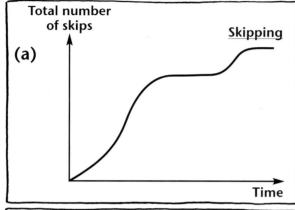

Total number of skips

Skipping

Time

(b)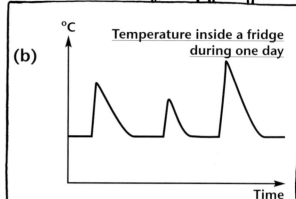

°C

Temperature inside a fridge during one day

Time

(c)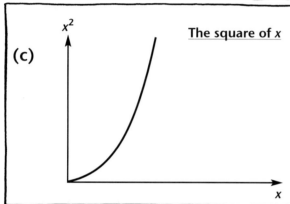

x^2

The square of x

x

(d)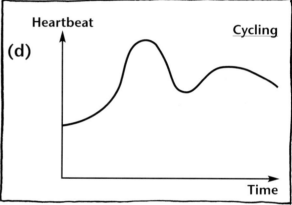

Heartbeat

Cycling

Time

(e)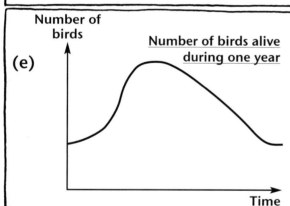

Number of birds

Number of birds alive during one year

Time

(f)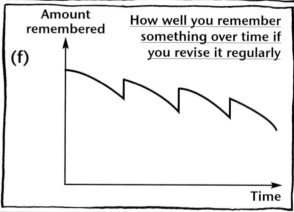

Amount remembered

How well you remember something over time if you revise it regularly

Time

B Sketch a line to show the temperature in your classroom during the day.

Compare your graph with a partner's. Discuss similarities and differences.

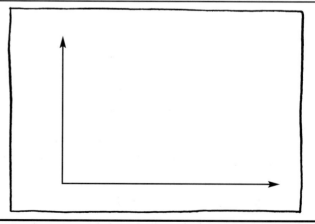

 Think carefully about each situation and try to imagine what could be happening to create a graph of that shape.

Developing Numeracy
Algebra
Year 9
© A & C BLACK

Explain that!

Plot graphs of
linear functions in
real-life situations

1. (a) Which graph do you think most appropriately matches the description? _____

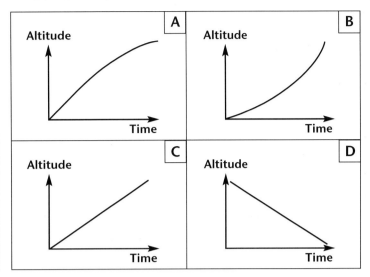

The altitude of an aeroplane during the first half hour after take-off.

(b) Discuss the graphs with a partner. Explain how you decided on your answer.

2. Sketch a line graph to match each description. Explain your graphs to a partner.

(a) The number of euros (€) you can buy for a given number of pounds (£).

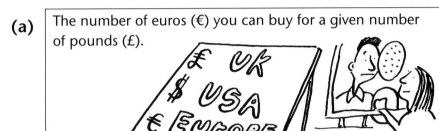

(b) The number of CDs sold as the price decreases.

(c) The height above ground of a carriage on a Big Wheel as the wheel revolves.

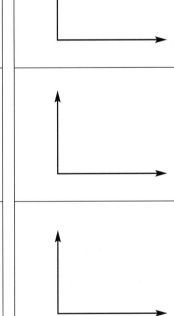

- Write a description of your activities during a P.E. lesson. Sketch a line graph of your heartbeat.
- Do you think your heartbeat will slow down at the same rate as it speeds up?

Think carefully about whether the line of each graph will grow more quickly/slowly at first, or whether it will grow at a constant rate.

Answers

p 8

A Values of x that meet the following criteria.
x could not be:

   (a) 7 or greater
   (b) 2 or less
   (c) less than $^-3$
   (d) more than $^-5$
   (e) zero or less, or greater than 1
   (f) less than $^-5$ or greater than $^-4$

B   **(a)** $y + 4 > 11$ True
    (b) $y - 3 \leq 1$ True
    (c) $y \geq 1$ True
    (d) $y + 10 > 6$ True
    (e) $y - 4 \leq {}^-3.5$ True

p 9

C1 **(a)** $2y > 12$ True
    (b) $5y \leq 20$ True
    (c) $\frac{y}{5} \geq 7$ True
    (d) $^-2y > {}^-10$ False
    (e) $^-y \leq {}^-2$ False
    (f) $-\frac{y}{4} \leq {}^-4$ False
    (g) $^-y \leq 1$ False

Now try this!
(a) $e > 9$ **(b)** $f \leq {}^-1$

p 10

A1 **(a)**

Value of a	2a + 8	3(a + 2)
1	10	9
2	12	12
3	14	15
4	16	18
5	18	21

   (b) 2

A2 **(a)**

Value of a	2(a + 3)	2a + 6
1	8	8
2	10	10
3	12	12
4	14	14
5	16	16

   (b) All of them

B   **(a)** Only when $y = 6$ are these two expressions equal.
    (b) Whatever the value of a is, these two expressions are equal.
    (c) Only when $x = 7$ are these two expressions equal.
    (d) Whatever the value of b is, these two expressions are equal.
    (e) Only when $s = 4$ are these two expressions equal.
    (f) Only when $p = 0$ are these two expressions equal.

p 11

C1 **(a)** Identically equal   **(f)** Identically equal
   (b) Not identically equal   **(g)** Not identically equal
   (c) Identically equal   **(h)** Identically equal
   (d) Not identically equal   **(i)** Identically equal
   (e) Identically equal   **(j)** Not identically equal

C2 $2(n + 1) \equiv 2n + 2$
    $4(n + 2) \equiv 4n + 8$
    $n \times n \times n \equiv n^3$
    $3(2n - n) \equiv 3n$
    $4(n + 1) \equiv 4n + 4$
    $3n + 0 \equiv 4n - n$

C3 Only true when:
    $n = 6$ $n = 2$
    $n = 3$ $n = 0$

p 12

A   **(a)** n^5
    (b) a^7
    (c) c^6
    (d) y^8
    (e) b^2
    (f) x^3
    (g) m
    (h) d^2

p 13

C2 **(a)** 3^5 **(b)** 7^5 **(c)** a
   (d) 9^4 **(e)** d^2 **(f)** x^4
   (g) 3^2 **(h)** 6   **(i)** 4^5
   (j) 2^7 **(k)** 8^3 **(l)** 5^4
   (m) 1   **(n)** a^7 **(o)** b^{-1}
   (p) c **(q)** y^{-1} **(r)** n^{-2}

Now try this!
Units digits of the powers of 4 alternate between 6 and 4.
Even number powers give 6, odd number powers give 4.

p 14

A1 **(a)** $3a + 3b$ **(b)** $5a + 20$ **(c)** $56 + 7b$
   (d) $xy + xz$ **(e)** $ab + 9a$ **(f)** $5a - 20$
   (g) $4x - 4y$ **(h)** $63 - 9b$ **(i)** $a^2 - 3a$

A2 **(a)** $3(a + 2)$ **(b)** $4(a + 2)$ **(c)** $5(d + 3e)$
   (d) $3(3c + 2d)$ **(e)** $2(x + 4y)$ **(f)** $10(p + q)$
   (g) $4(a - 3b)$ **(h)** $x(x - 1)$ **(i)** $2(5s - 4t)$
   (j) $5x(3 - x)$ **(k)** $6(t - 1)$ **(l)** $2g(4 - 9g)$

B   **(a)** $11a + 10b$ **(b)** $14c + 17d$
       $^-5a + 2b$ $^-6c + 7d$
    (c) $17x - 7y$ **(d)** $19s + t$
       $^-7x - 23y$ $5s + 29t$
    (e) $18a - 33b$ **(f)** $39m - 28n$
       $^-6a - 27b$ $^-9m + 8n$

p 15

C1 **(a)** $2x + 8$ **(b)** $x^2 + 2x$ **(c)** $6x + 9$
   (d) $x^2 - 3x$ **(e)** $12x - 36$ **(f)** $3x^2 - 7x$
   (g) $2x^2 + 12x$ **(h)** $6x^2 + 6x$ **(i)** $20x^2 - 30x$

C2 **(a)** $x + 6$ **(b)** $x + 1$ **(c)** $x + 2$
   (d) $x + 4$ **(e)** $2x - 1$ **(f)** $3x - 2$

p 16

A1 **(a)** 42   **(b)** 28   **(c)** 24
   (d) 35   **(e)** 90   **(f)** 36
   (g) ab **(h)** cd **(i)** ef

A2 **(a)** $\frac{12}{42}$ **(b)** $\frac{21}{28}$ **(c)** $\frac{30}{35}$
   (d) $\frac{28}{36}$ **(e)** $\frac{2b}{ab}$ **(f)** $\frac{3a}{ab}$
   (g) $\frac{7d}{cd}$ **(h)** $\frac{c}{cd}$ **(i)** $\frac{a^2}{ab}$

B   **(a)** $\frac{7}{8}$
    (b) $\frac{27}{35}$
    (c) $1\frac{1}{24}$
    (d) $\frac{17}{20}$
    (e) $\frac{(b + 2a)}{ab}$
    (f) $\frac{(2d + 3c)}{cd}$

p 17

C1 **(a)** $\frac{(3b - a)}{ab}$
    (b) $\frac{(4b + 3a)}{ab}$
    (c) $\frac{(5d + 2c)}{cd}$
    (d) $\frac{(6d - 3c)}{cd}$
    (e) $\frac{(ad + bc)}{cd}$
    (f) $\frac{(ad - bc)}{cd}$

Now try this!
(a) $\frac{(ad + ac)}{cd}$ $\frac{(ad - ac)}{cd}$
(b) $\frac{(2bd + bc)}{cd}$ $\frac{(2bd - bc)}{cd}$
(c) $\frac{(d^2 + c^2)}{cd}$ $\frac{(d^2 - c^2)}{cd}$

p 18

A Proof to show that expressions can be simplified to:
- (a) $3(n + 1)$
- (b) $5(n + 2)$
- (c) $7(n + 3)$
- (d) $2n + 1$

B Each expression below can be simplified to n:
- (a) $\frac{2(n + 5) - 8}{2} - 1$
- (b) $\frac{4(n - 1) + 12}{4} - 2$
- (c) $\frac{2(5n - 1) + 2}{10}$
- (d) $\left(\frac{6(n + 4) - 20}{2} - 2\right) \div 3$

p 19

C2
- (a) $48 - 3n$
  $6(8 - n) + 3n$
  $24 + 3(8 - n)$
- (b) $45 - 4n$
  $5(9 - n) + n$
  $9 + 4(9 - n)$
- (c) $66 - 4n$
  $6(11 - n) + 2n$
  $22 + 4(11 - n)$
- (d) $35 - 5n$
  $7(5 - n) + 2n$
  $10 + 5(5 - n)$

Now try this!
$(2n + 1)^2 = 4n(n + 1) + 1$

p 20

A
- (a) $^-3$
- (b) $^-2$
- (c) 4
- (d) 1
- (e) $^-5$
- (f) 10
- (g) $^-6$
- (h) $^-7$
- (i) $^-5$
- (j) $^-3$
- (k) $^-2$
- (l) $^-9$

B
- (a) $19, 20, 21, 22$
- (b) $34, 35, 36$
- (c) $26, 27, 28, 29, 30$
- (d) $^-41, ^-40, ^-39, ^-38, ^-37$

p 21

C1
- (a) 3
- (b) $^-2$
- (c) $^-3$
- (d) $^-5$
- (e) 4
- (f) $^-4$
- (g) 2
- (h) $^-9$

C2 (a) $a = 4, b = ^-5, c = ^-1$

Now try this!

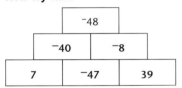

p 22

A
- (a) 11
- (b) 8
- (c) 10
- (d) 15

B
- (a) Tim 21, Bill 30, Doug 16
- (b) Tim 17, Bill 20, Doug 10
- (c) Tim 16, Bill 10, Doug 24
- (d) Tim 18, Bill 10, Doug 14

p 23

C1
- (a) $88°, 44°, 48°$
- (b) $47°, 26°, 107°$
- (c) $77°, 60°, 43°$
- (d) $54°, 60°, 66°$

C2
- (a) $53°, 48°, 79°$
- (b) $40°, 86°, 54°$
- (c) $210°, 76°, 74°$
- (d) $120°, 86°, 110°, 44°$
- (e) $126°, 95°, 100°, 39°$

Now try this!
- (a) $36°, 72°, 108°, 144°$
- (b) $30°, 150°, 120°, 60°$
- (c) $45°, 67.5°, 112.5°, 135°$

p 24

A (a)

Starting number	Amy's answer	Jamie's answer
5	17	13
6	20	17
7	23	21

(b) $x = 9$

B
- (a) 2
- (b) 4
- (c) 5
- (d) $^-2$
- (e) $^-4$
- (f) 6
- (g) $^-9$
- (h) $^-3$

p 25

C1
- (a) $x = 2$ Length of side = 10 cm
- (b) $x = 18$ Length of side = 60 cm
- (c) $x = 4$ Length of side = 24 cm
- (d) $x = 3$ Length of side = 32 cm
- (e) $x = 6$ Length of side = 4 cm
- (f) $x = 2$ Length of side = 1.5 cm

C2
- (a) 56 cm
- (b) 126 cm
- (c) 63 cm
- (d) 75.25 cm
- (e) 98 cm
- (f) 243 cm

Now try this!
198

p 26

A (a) $x(x + 5)$

x	$x + 5$	$x(x + 5)$
5	10	50
6	11	66
5.6	10.6	59.36
5.65	10.65	60.1725
5.64	10.64	60.0096
5.63	10.63	59.8469

(b) $x(11 - x)$

x	$11 - x$	$x(11 - x)$
4	7	28
5	6	30
4.5	6.5	29.25
4.4	6.6	29.04
4.39	6.61	29.0179
4.38	6.62	28.9956

(c) $x(x + 0.8)$

x	$x + 0.8$	$x(x + 0.8)$
2.7	3.5	9.45
2.6	3.4	8.84
2.65	3.45	9.1425
2.64	3.44	9.0816
2.63	3.43	9.0209
2.62	3.42	8.9604

(d) $x(8.6 - x)$

x	$8.6 - x$	$x(8.6 - x)$
8	0.6	4.8
7.9	0.7	5.53
7.95	0.65	5.1675
7.96	0.64	5.0944
7.97	0.63	5.0211
7.98	0.62	4.9476

(e) $x(x + 19)$

x	$x + 19$	$x(x + 19)$
1	20	20
0	19	0
0.5	19.5	9.75
0.6	19.6	11.76
0.52	19.52	10.1504
0.51	19.51	9.9501

(f) $x(9.1 - x)$

x	$9.1 - x$	$x(9.1 - x)$
3	6.1	18.3
4	5.1	20.4
3.7	5.4	19.98
3.8	5.3	20.14
3.72	5.38	20.0136
3.71	5.39	19.9969

B x must be between:
- **(a)** 5.63 and 5.64
- **(b)** 4.38 and 4.39
- **(c)** 2.62 and 2.63
- **(d)** 7.97 and 7.98
- **(e)** 0.51 and 0.52
- **(f)** 3.71 and 3.72

p 27
C
(a) Length: 8.56 cm	Width: 4.56 cm
(b) Length: 9.93 cm	Width: 3.93 cm
(c) Length: 11.42 cm	Width: 3.42 cm
(d) Length: 7.92 cm	Width: 4.92 cm

Now try this!
28, 29, 30

p 28
A1
- **(a)** ±9
- **(b)** ±6
- **(c)** ±13
- **(d)** ±5
- **(e)** ±1.3
- **(f)** 5, ⁻9
- **(g)** 2, ⁻6
- **(h)** 5.5, ⁻7.5
- **(i)** 8, ⁻6
- **(j)** 2, ⁻10
- **(k)** ±3
- **(l)** ±4

A2
- **(a)** 4
- **(b)** 4.5
- **(c)** 8.5
- **(d)** 3
- **(e)** 1.8
- **(f)** 4.2

B2 4.57

p 29
C1
- **(a)** $y = 4.23$
- **(b)** $n = 8.31$
- **(c)** $m = 3.87$

C2
- **(b)** Length: 8.65 cm
  Width: 2.65 cm

Now try this!
- **(a)** $x = 7.75$
- **(b)** $c = 8.85$
- **(c)** $m = 6.95$

p 30
A1
- **(a)** $y = $ 4.5, 9, 13.5, 18, 22.5, 27, 31.5, 36, 40.5, 45
- **(b)** As x increases by equal amounts, y increases by equal amounts.

A2 (b) and (c)

A3 Yes

B1
- **(a)** $y = $ 25, 50, 75, 100, 125, 150, 175, 200, 225, 250
- **(b)** $\frac{25}{1}, \frac{50}{2}, \frac{75}{3}, \frac{100}{4}, \frac{125}{5}, \frac{150}{6}, \frac{175}{7}, \frac{200}{8}, \frac{225}{9}, \frac{250}{10}$
- **(c)** The number is always 25.
- **(d)** Yes

B2 **(a)** $y = 4x$, $y = \frac{x}{2}$

p 31
C1
- **(a)** $y = $ 7.9, 15.8, 23.7, 31.6, 39.5, 47.4, 55.3, 63.2, 71.1, 79
- **(b)** $\frac{7.9}{1}, \frac{15.8}{2}, \frac{23.7}{3}, \frac{31.6}{4}, \frac{39.5}{5}, \frac{47.4}{6}, \frac{55.3}{7}, \frac{63.2}{8}, \frac{71.1}{9}, \frac{79}{10}$
- **(c)** 7.9

C2
- **(a)** £55.30
- **(b)** 71.1 m
- **(c)** 47.4 cm

C3
- **(a)** 135 ml
- **(b)** 763 ml
- **(c)** 228 ml
- **(d)** 182 ml

Now try this!
$a = 8.4$ cm, $b = 4.35$ cm

p 32
A
- **(a)** 4
- **(b)** 9
- **(c)** 6.01
- **(d)** 60
- **(e)** ⁻16
- **(f)** 30
- **(g)** ⁻16
- **(h)** ⁻2
- **(i)** 96
- **(j)** 0.606

B Code:
- **(a)** NAME
- **(b)** TWO
- **(c)** CARS

p 33
C Code:
- **(a)** WHO
- **(b)** WAS
- **(c)** THE
- **(d)** FIRST
- **(e)** MAN
- **(f)** IN
- **(g)** SPACE

p 34
A1
- **(a)** 41 °F
- **(b)** 59 °F
- **(c)** 68 °F
- **(d)** 77 °F
- **(e)** 14 °F
- **(f)** ⁻22 °F
- **(g)** 63 °F
- **(h)** 73 °F
- **(i)** 90 °F
- **(j)** 99 °F
- **(k)** 106 °F
- **(l)** 111 °F
- **(m)** ⁻8 °F
- **(n)** ⁻11 °F
- **(o)** ⁻18 °F

A2
- **(a)** 10 °C
- **(b)** 35 °C
- **(c)** 40 °C
- **(d)** ⁻5 °C
- **(e)** ⁻15 °C
- **(f)** ⁻25 °C
- **(g)** 0 °C
- **(h)** 8 °C
- **(i)** 12 °C
- **(j)** 15 °C
- **(k)** 18 °C
- **(l)** 24 °C
- **(m)** 28 °C
- **(n)** ⁻29 °C
- **(o)** ⁻31 °C

B $F = \frac{9}{5}(C + 40) - 40$

p 35
C1 **(a)**

°C	⁻50	⁻35	⁻30	⁻10	0	10	20	30
°F	⁻58	⁻31	⁻22	14	32	50	68	86

- **(b)** Possible answers:
  ⁻30 °C, ⁻22 °F ⁻35 °C, ⁻31 °F
  ⁻10 °C, 14 °F 0 °C, 32 °F
  10 °C, 50 °F 20 °C, 68 °F
  30 °C, 86 °F
- **(c)** ⁻50 °C, ⁻58 °F

C2
- **(a)** $F = ⁻40°$
- **(b)** 5 °F
- **(c)** ⁻130 °F

Now try this!
$F = \frac{9}{5}C + 72 - 40 = \frac{9}{5}C + 32$
$C = \frac{5}{9}(F - 32)$

p 36
A
$$R = \frac{V}{I}$$
$$d = \frac{C}{\pi}$$
$$r = \frac{C}{2\pi}$$
$$u = v - at$$
$$l = \frac{P}{2} - w$$
$$h = \frac{V}{lb}$$
$$a = \frac{(v - u)}{t}$$
$$h = \frac{2A}{b}$$
$$r = \frac{p}{(\pi + 2)}$$
$$b = \frac{2A}{h} - a$$
$$a = \frac{F}{m}$$
$$d = \sqrt{s}$$
$$r = \sqrt{\left(\frac{A}{\pi}\right)}$$
$$h = \frac{V}{\pi r^2}$$
$$a = \sqrt{\left(\frac{S}{3}\right)}$$
$$l = \sqrt[3]{A}$$
$$r = \sqrt[3]{\left(\frac{3V}{4\pi}\right)}$$

B (a) $V = lbh$
(b) $P = 2(l + w)$
(c) $A = \frac{1}{2}bh$
(d) $A = \pi r^2$
(e) $V = \pi r^2 h$
(f) $A = \frac{1}{2}h(a + b)$

p 37
C1 $b = \frac{A}{\pi a}$
C2 (a) 2.5 cm   (b) 5.8 cm
     (c) 6.1 cm   (d) 6.3 cm
C3 $r = \sqrt{\frac{V}{\pi h}}$
C4 (a) 1.1 cm   (b) 1.3 cm   (c) 2.1 cm
     (d) 1.8 cm   (e) 1.8 cm   (f) 1.6 cm

Now try this!
(a) $l = g\left(\frac{T}{2\pi}\right)^2$ (b) $w = 5R^2 - l$ (c) $t = \sqrt{\left(\frac{s}{5} + u\right)}$

p 38
A1 (a) $m = 40x + 20$ (c) $70x + 35$
     (b) $40x + 20$ (d) $50x + 25$
A2 (a) 3 hrs 40 mins
     (b) 2 hrs 40 mins
     (c) 7 hrs
     (d) 12 hrs 15 mins
B1 $c = 9.9m + 8.5$
B2 (a) $c = 11m + 6.2$ (b) $c = 5.2m + 9.5$
B3 (a) Chit-chat   (b) Chit-chat   (c) Chit-chat

p 39
C1 (a) 1, 4, 16, 36, 64, 100, 400
     (b) $L = \frac{1}{2}T^2$
C2 (a) 2, 8, 32, 72, 128, 199, 801
     (b) $T^2 = 4L$

Now try this!
5 seconds

p 40
A (a) 15, 10, 5, 0, $^-$5, $^-$10
     (b) 18, 14, 10, 6, 2, $^-$2
     (c) 5, 8, 11, 14, 17, 20
     (d) 3, 7, 11, 15, 19, 23
     (e) 3, 9, 15, 21, 27, 33
     (f) 12, 5, $^-$2, $^-$9, $^-$16, $^-$23
     (g) 20, 24, 28, 32, 36, 40
     (h) $^-$12, $^-$9, $^-$6, $^-$3, 0, 3

B

Sequence	(a)	(b)	(c)	(d)	(e)	(f)	(g)	(h)
10th term	$^-$30	$^-$18	32	39	57	$-$51	56	15
20th term	$^-$80	$^-$58	62	79	117	$^-$121	96	45
100th term	$^-$480	$^-$378	302	399	597	$^-$681	416	285

p 42
A (a) $a = 2$
     $b = 3$
     First term = 5
     Difference between adjacent terms = 2
     (b) $a = 6$
     $b = 5$
     First term = 11
     Difference between adjacent terms = 6
     (c) $a = 2$
     $b = ^-7$
     First term = $^-5$
     Difference between adjacent terms = 2

(d) $a = 5$
     $b = 8$
     First term = 13
     Difference between adjacent terms = 5
(e) $a = \frac{1}{2}$
     $b = ^-1.5$
     First term = $^-1$
     Difference between adjacent terms = 0.5
B First term = $a + b$
     Difference between adjacent terms = a

p 43
C1 (a) $a = 5$
     $b = ^-3$
     First term = 2
     Difference between adjacent terms = 5
     (b) The first term is equal to $a + b$.
     The difference between adjacent terms is the same
     as a.

Now try this!
(a) $n - \frac{1}{2}$
(b) $2n + 4$

p 44
A1 (a) $2n^2 + 3$, $5n + 3$
     (b) $4n^2 + 2$, $4n + 2$
     (c) $5n - 3$, $3n^2 - 1$
     (d) $n^2 - n$, $2(n - 1)$
     (e) $6n^2 - 10$, $4n - 8$
B (a) 1, 4, 9, 16, 25, 36   (b) 4, 7, 12, 19, 28, 39
     (c) $^-1$, 2, 7, 14, 23, 34   (d) 2, 8, 18, 32, 50, 72
     (e) 4, 10, 20, 34, 52, 74   (f) $^-1$, 5, 15, 29, 47, 69

p 45
C1 Second difference:
     (a) 2
     (b) 4
     (c) 6
     (d) 8
     (e) 8
C2 The second difference is twice the number of n^2.

Now try this!
(a) $3n^2 + 1$ (b) $4n^2 + 2$
(c) $n^2 - 2$ (d) $2n^2 + 10$

p 46
A1

Shape number (n)	1	2	3	4	5	6
Number of grey squares	1	1	1	1	1	1
Number of white squares	2	4	6	8	10	12
Total number of squares	3	5	7	9	11	13

A2 (a) Multiples of 2, starting with 2
     (b) Always 1
     (c) Consecutive odd numbers, starting with 3
A3 (a) 1
     (b) 200
A4 $2n + 1$
B1

Shape number (n)	1	2	3	4	5	6
Number of grey squares	2	2	2	2	2	2
Number of white squares	6	12	18	24	30	36
Total number of squares	8	14	20	26	32	38

B2 (a) Multiples of 6, starting with 6
     (b) Always 2
     (c) Increases by 6, starting from 8

B3 (a) 2

(b) 600

B4 $6n + 2$

p 47

C1 (a) Second difference: 2

(b) n^2

C2 (a) Second difference: 4

(b) $2n^2$

C3 $3n^2$

Now try this!

0, 1, 3, 6, 10, 15

Triangular numbers

Rule: $\frac{1}{2}(n^2 - n)$

p 48

A (a) $2n + 1$

(b) $2n + 3$

(c) $3n + 1$

(d) $4n + 1$

(e) $2n + 2$

B2 (a) $3n + 3$ (b) $4n + 2$

(c) $2n + 4$ (d) $3n + 5$

(e) $4n + 3$ (f) $3n + 2$

p 49

C1 (b) Second difference: 2

C2 (b) Second difference: 1

Now try this!

One sequence is half the other.

p 50

A1 (a) 1, 3, 5, 7, 9, 11 (b) $^-2$, 1, 4, 7, 10, 13

A2 (b) $^-1$, 2, 5, 8, 11, 14

(d) $x \longrightarrow \frac{(x + 1)}{3}$

B1 (a) $x \longrightarrow \frac{(x - 1)}{2}$ (b) $x \longrightarrow \frac{(x + 2)}{3}$

(c) $x \longrightarrow 2(x + 5)$ (d) $x \longrightarrow \frac{x}{6} - 4$

(e) $x \longrightarrow \frac{(x - 4)}{8}$ (f) $x \longrightarrow \frac{(x + 3)}{7}$

p 51

C2 (b) Yes

C3 (b) Yes

(c) Yes

C4 (a) $x \longrightarrow 7 - x$ (b) $x \longrightarrow \frac{(5 - x)}{2}$

(c) $x \longrightarrow 4(x - 5)$ (d) $x \longrightarrow 2x + 2$

(e) $x \longrightarrow 4 - \frac{x}{3}$ (f) $x \longrightarrow 3x - 4$

(g) $x \longrightarrow 5x + 3$

Now try this!

$x \longrightarrow 7 - x$

p 52

A1 $y + 2x - 1 = 0$ $y = 1 - 2x$

$y - x + 2 = 0$ $y = x - 2$

$y - 2x + 1 = 0$ $y = 2x - 1$

$y + 2x - 2 = 0$ $y = 2 - 2x$

$y - x - 1 = 0$ $y = x + 1$

A2 (a) $y = 5 - 3x$ (b) $y = 4x + 6$

(c) $y = 2x - 4$ (d) $y = ^-2 - 6x$

(e) $y = 5x + 1$ (f) $y = 9 - 8x$

B1 (a) $y = 5 - 2x$

(b) 11, 9, 7, 5, 3, 1, $^-1$

B2 (b) (0, 5)

B3 (a) 5

(b) $^-2$

B4 Left

p 53

C1 (a) $y = 3x$ (b) $y = 4x$

(c) $y = ^-5x$ (d) $y = 7x - 3$

(e) $y = 4x + 5$ (f) $y = 2 - 7x$

(g) $y = \frac{(13 + x)}{2}$ (h) $y = \frac{(8 - 3x)}{2}$

(i) $y = \frac{(x - 6)}{2}$ (j) $y = \frac{(2 - 5x)}{4}$

(k) $y = \frac{(^-5 - 2x)}{3}$ (l) $y = \frac{(4x + 3)}{5}$

C3 (a) The value of the constant

(b) Positive or negative number of x

(c) The larger the number x is multiplied by, the steeper the gradient

p 54

A (a) $\frac{1}{3}$

(b) 1

(c) 3

B1 (a) $y = 2x - 3$ (b) $y = 3x + 4$

(c) $y = 4x - 1$ (d) $y = 5x + 2$

B2 (a) $^-9, ^-7, ^-5, ^-3, ^-1, 1, 3$ (b) $^-5, ^-2, 1, 4, 7, 10, 13$

(c) $^-13, ^-9, ^-5, ^-1, 3, 7, 11$ (d) $^-13, ^-8, ^-3, 2, 7, 12, 17$

B4 (a) 2 (b) 3 (c) 4 (d) 5

p 55

C1 (a) $y = x$ (b) $y = 2x - 3$

(c) $y = ^-x$ (d) $y = ^-2x + 3$

(e) $y = ^-4x + 2$ (f) $y = ^-6x - 2$

C2 (a) $^-3, ^-2, ^-1, 0, 1, 2, 3$ (b) $^-9, ^-7, ^-5, ^-3, ^-1, 1, 3$

(c) $3, 2, 1, 0, ^-1, ^-2, ^-3$ (d) $9, 7, 5, 3, 1, ^-1, ^-3$

(e) $14, 10, 6, 2, ^-2, ^-6, ^-10$ (f) $16, 10, 4, ^-2, ^-8, ^-14, ^-20$

C4 (a) 1 (b) 2 (c) $^-1$

(d) $^-2$ (e) $^-4$ (f) $^-6$

Now try this!

(a) $y = 4x - 2$ (b) $y = ^-3x + 7$

p 56

A1 A B

D C

p 59

C1 (a) A

64